# SET FREE

## WHOM THE SON SETS FREE IS FREE INDEED

Candice Irene

**To order additional copies of this book, contact:**
Xlibris
844-714-8691
www.Xlibris.com
Orders@Xlibris.com
814099

This love book is written by Candice Irene as a thank you to our amazing Father God Almighty, our Lord and Savior, the Holy Spirit, and the host of guardian angels for an incredible feat of saving the world from evil; at the appointed time.

***This is a unique writing. It is not really written in a typical book form with a beginning, middle, and end, but more as a Holy Spirit downloading to my inner being as food for my soul. I felt led by the Holy Spirit to type particular Scriptures that would feed my inner being a spiritual uplifting. Once I type the Holy Spirit downloading messages that I feel inspired to type, I then read them, in print, as often as necessary to refresh my heart, mind, and soul. They become like a daily meal that nourishes my entire being. I am able to ingest all that I feel led to type. It stays with me and becomes part of me, plus I can share my writings with others.

***All quotes in this book were taken from the New King James Version (NKJV) unless otherwise indicated. All Bible quotes are in italics.

***All capital letters used in the book such as LORD are to denote reference to God Almighty. All small letters except the first letter are used in reference to Jesus Christ as such: Lord.

# CONTENTS

# Preface

Upon completion of this thirty-day April 2020 writing, I had four very important and special people in my life help me edit it and give their opinions as they were reading it. They all had different outlooks on the same material.

My sister Sandy, who is also my best friend, says she would like to have permission to turn it into a "how-to" book. We both agree that the key to being set free from the demonic attacks of the enemy is to have Bible Scripture embedded in your mind, so when the enemy tries to deceive us, simply know the Scripture that will make him a liar. This book clearly demonstrates how I did that. This love book is written from my heart to your heart. It took thirty days in the month of April 2020 to write this book. It was written during the most unusual time that our present-day world has ever known, which is the pandemic of the Coronavirus or COVID-19. I know God wanted the four of us to remain very grounded during this time and trust in Him completely, which I did and I do. Amen.

My dear lifetime friend Linda says it should be published as a thirty-day devotional and she showed me a couple of hers so I could comprehend what she was speaking of. Linda is always encouraging and says whatever you want to call it, just make sure you get it published because people need to read this. She always says, "Make sure I get a few extra copies because I have some loved ones that I want to read this, right away." I always appreciate her heartfelt encouragement.

My friend Tom says, all my writings are like a thesis paper written for a possible doctoral degree as college students write when they are trying to further their degree. He said they are more like a research-dissertation style of writing. Tom is, and was, always encouraging. Tom always expresses how amazed he is by my biblical knowledge and my devoted relationship with God, Jesus, and how I always seemed to hear the Holy Spirit from on high.

Last but not least my friend Richard, who is my sister's brother-in-law, says about all my writings, "Candice, it's your book and you have to write it the way that you feel God is leading you to write it." He does not change anything but makes sure all the punctuation and sentence structure is correct.

I am very grateful to have the four of them for encouragement, love, and support in all my endeavors. When God allows or sends certain people in your life, I know it is not by accident as my very first book is about that very happening. I titled my first book written and published *Not By Accident,* with a subtitle of "Coins and People with a Purpose." It was a fun book to write and also my *Genesis book* of how I began to acknowledge and then learn how to hear God with His still small silent voice, yet speaking in volumes to my heart, mind, and soul.

By writing all seven books, I got to know God as my Father God, Jesus as my Lord and Savior, plus my very best friend and confidant, the Holy Spirit as my tutor, guide, helper, my whisper in the wind, and so much more. I am aware of the guardian angels' presence, and I always call on them through Psalm 91:11 when I am in immediate need or when I feel someone else is; most assuredly I call on them whenever I hear sirens. I like to call the guardian angels as a lot of people need to call 911 for an ambulance or a police interaction. I call 9111 in prayer often because it reminds me of immediate assistance, like the number 911 is for all of the world's immediate helpline number. Psalm 91:11 says, *"For He shall give His angels charge over you."* God always sends as many guardian angels that I need to handle whatever is causing me any harm, trouble, or discomfort. I am thankful I learned to call 9111 in prayer, God's guardian angels help team, when I am in need of immediate assistance, or if one of my family members, friends, acquaintances, etc. is in need of help. Grateful indeed am I to know so many Scriptures to call upon when I am in need. They are my lifeline to the Creator of the universe and to that fact I do want to shout hallelujah.

***Tom Reed writes this about the book: "Candice, you have a literary mind in the English language. Your writing is eye-opening. I think your friend Linda discovered that too. I think she and I are on the same page that you ascertained a special gift of how to express your love for God, Jesus, and the Holy Spirit, and that you are willing to share your gift with anyone that is willing to listen. I am inspired so much by the way you delivered your amazing writings about God and Jesus. It simply makes me speechless. I think your writing comes from deep within your heart."

# Introduction

This book was written at the height of the worldwide pandemic of the COVID-19 virus. This is the first time that this generation and, for that matter, the New Testament world has ever faced such a time as this. I knew in my heart that our Father God wanted to help me stay calm, at peace, and have complete faith in Him. I truly feel at this time I am doing just that. God's Holy Spirit prompted me to write this book on our stay-at-home ordinance issued by President Trump in order to try to keep the world safe from the spreading of the contagious virus.

I believe the Holy Spirit knows exactly how to keep me fortified and full of faith whenever something that is not of God could be lurking. It seems every single time something is brewing, the LORD'S Holy Spirit brings Scripture to mind and I immediately take note of it usually by writing and/or typing. Quieting my mind and tuning out the phone, television, etc. brings me to a peace that does indeed surpass all understanding as written in Philippians 4:7, which says *"And the peace of God, which surpasses all understanding, will guard your hearts and minds through Christ Jesus."* So that is why my Father God and your Father God's Holy Spirit within all believers' hearts, minds, and souls had me write this book. It fortified me by the blood of Jesus; I hope it does the same for you in this pandemic-demonic time caused by Satan and his demonic co-workers. I want each and every person alive to realize this does not take God Almighty, Creator of the world, by surprise for He is omniscient, omnipresent, and omnipotent, so I know and I hope you too know you are covered by the blood of Jesus and you have no reason to lose your peace at a time such as this. Just do as it says to do in 1 Peter 5:8, which goes: *"Be sober, be vigilant, because your adversary the devil walks about like a roaring lion, seeking whom he may devour."* I am most assuredly looking forward to the day when Revelation 20:10 is fulfilled: *"And the devil who deceived them was thrown into the lake of fire and brimstone, where the beast and the false prophet are also . . ."* To that revelation written and soon being fulfilled, I do want to shout, amen and hallelujah. However, in the mean-time I have made the choice to be like Joshua and do what the LORD commanded Joshua to do in Joshua 1:9, *"Have I not commanded you? Be strong and of good courage; do not be afraid, nor be dismayed, for the LORD your God is with you wherever you go."* Amen to those facts written and comforting all who choose to believe what is written in the Holy Bible; I pray in the name of Jesus that you take the time to read God's Holy Word, study it, believe it with all your heart, all your mind, all your soul, all your strength, and then sing praise and worship to our amazing heavenly family forevermore!

## RELEASED FROM CAPTIVITY
April 1, 2020, 6:59 a.m.

I have never felt this free in all my life. Every word written in the Holy Scripture is a fact. I am living proof. Every single Scripture I know and quote back to the Lord when I am in a situation comes to fruition. I am now sixty-four years alive. I would not change a thing because our Father God, who is the Most High above all creation, has delivered me and set me free even in this fallen world of chaos and unbelief.

Once I made the choice to believe and accept Jesus Christ as my Lord and Savior, and made my heavenly family my first priority, things unfolded for me just like a butterfly coming out of its cocoon. The LORD allowed me to experience everything—and I do mean everything—but then at just the right timing, I was called out of the worldly way of thinking. I believe I am on the right path because I trust God with all my heart, mind, soul, and strength, and it says in Proverbs 3:5–6, if we will trust the LORD with all our heart, He will direct our paths. I believe I am allowing God Almighty to direct my paths, at least I pray in the name of Jesus that I am, amen. I have been fully and completely transformed as written about in 2 Corinthians 5:14–21, *"For the love of Christ compels us, because we judge thus; that if One died for all, then all died; 15 and He died for all, that those who live should live no longer for themselves, but for Him who died for them and rose again. 16 Therefore, from now on, we regard no one according to the flesh. Even though we have known Christ according to the flesh, yet now we know Him thus no longer. 17 Therefore, if anyone is in Christ, he is a new creation; old things have passed away behold, all things have become*

1

*new. 18 Now all things are of God, who has reconciled us to Himself through Jesus Christ and has given us the ministry of reconciliation, 19 that is, that God was in Christ reconciling the world to Himself, not imputing their trespasses to them, and has committed us the word of reconciliation. 20 Now then, we are ambassadors for Christ, as though God were pleading through us: we implore you on Christ's behalf, be reconciled to God. 21 For He made Him who knew no sin to be sin for us, that we might become the righteousness of God in Him."* I am grateful beyond words to express my gratitude. Also when I read a little further in 2 Corinthians, I could feel my body soar with zeal, love, and passion for our LORD like the butterfly that is released into the world as a new creation and is no longer crawling on the ground of this world as a caterpillar but is made brand new after a time enclosed in a cocoon. I am new in my thinking after a time of believing the false pleasures of this world's way of thinking could fulfill me. There is no other substitute for the enveloping love of our heavenly family!

I absolutely feel so loved by our Father; His Son Jesus, who is our Lord and Savior; the Holy Spirit within; and the host of guardian angels keeping us safe and free from Satan's demonic fallen angels. There are many of them, but God has more guardian angels than Satan's team of fallen angels. Amen and hallelujah, for that fact is written about in Revelation 12:4! When I read in 2 Corinthians how one can be called out of the darkness and into communion with God's glory light just by making that personal choice of accepting Jesus, I knew that I was called and I harkened to the call and said, "Yes, Father, I want to be reconciled to you and become an ambassador for Your sake. Help me and I will." That is all it took and then I received 2 Corinthians 6:16–18, *"As God has said: 'I will dwell in them and walk among them. I will be their God, and they shall be My people.' 17 'Therefore come out from among them and be separate', says the Lord. 'Do not touch what is unclean, and I will receive you.' 18 'I will be a Father to you, and you shall be My sons and daughters,' says the LORD Almighty."* Wow, that is quite a new life with the LORD—my Father God looking out for me, His daughter, as I am a mother looking out for my beloved son, Garrett. Wow, Father God has given me this new life, and in return I want to be the best I can be for my heavenly family because of His goodness, mercy, grace, and overflowing love for all that will receive it. I do. How about you? This day, just say,

*"Father God, I believe You allowed Your Son to dwell among us as an example and then be crucified as a substitute for our sinful ways, and to pay our sin debt in full. I ask You, Father God Almighty, to help me become the person You created me to be. Help me come to know You and Your only-begotten Son and put Your Holy Spirit within me so I can be intimately connected to You forevermore and this I do ask in the Holy Name of Your begotten Son, Jesus Christ."* Loved ones, that is all it takes as long as your heart is sincere and then trust me, He will step in and your life will never be the same; you too will live Hallelujah Days, which I call the nine fruits of the Spirit listed in Galatians 5:22–23, *"Love, joy, peace, longsuffering, kindness, goodness, faithfulness, gentleness, and self-control."*

**I HAVE BEEN SET FREE BY THE BLOOD OF JESUS**
Blessed indeed are all who believe and are set free
April 2, 2020, 7:31 a.m.

I have been set free by the blood of Jesus. John says in verse 8:36, *"Whom the Son sets free is free indeed."* (NIV) Amen. As I sat with the Lord this morning, I recognized Him in all my life endeavors and now I know to thank Him. Before I came to know my Lord and Savior, I kind of thought I was winging it and then by luck I was scoring high in my job/career, my finances, the selection of my home, my friends, etc. But now, every morning since the age of fifty, known as "my jubilee year," I realize it was my Father God's Holy Spirit abiding in me, prompting me all along in all my ways. How blessed am I that He would stand with me when I didn't even know Him intimately? How blessed indeed are we who come to know Him just by asking and then seeking as written in Matthew 7:7–8, *"Ask, and it will be given to you; seek, and you will find; knock, and it will be opened to you. 8 For everyone who asks receives, and he who seeks finds, and to him who knocks it will be opened."* Our heavenly family is amazing, phenomenal, patient, steadfast, and never giving up on wanting to rescue us, and it even says in Luke 15:7, *"I tell you in the same way, there will be more joy in heaven over one sinner who repents than over ninety-nine righteous persons who need no repentance."* This is similar to Luke 15:10, *"In the same way, I tell you, there is joy in the presence of the angels of God over one sinner who repents."* When we finally realize we have been set free from bondage and the scheming of the evil ones, I believe the rejoicing is almost unfathomable. Amen! I know the joy of Jesus within my heart, mind, and soul is almost beyond belief. This, indeed, is the best it can be on this fallen earth, but those who endure to the end will be in constant never-ending amazement of how good our Father God Almighty and His only begotten Son truly are! Matthew 24:13–15 says, *"But he who endures to the end shall be saved. 14 And this gospel of the kingdom will be preached in all the world as a witness to all the nations, and then the end will come. 15 Therefore when you see the 'abomination of desolation,' spoken of by Daniel the prophet, standing in the holy place ('Whoever reads, let him understand')."*

Our Father God and Jesus promised not to leave us as orphans to fend for ourselves but instead sent us the Holy Spirit to abide in us forevermore. That is phenomenal! John 14:16–20 says, *"And I will pray the Father, and He will give you another helper, that He may abide with you forever; 17 the Spirit of truth, whom the world cannot receive, because it neither sees Him nor knows Him; but you know Him, for He dwells with you and will be in you. 18 I will not leave you orphans; I will come to you. 19 A little while longer and the world will see Me no more, but you will see Me. Because I live, you will live also. 20 At that day you will know that I am in My Father, and you in Me, and I in you."* How grateful I am to learn what I have learned because I said, "Yes, I want Jesus Christ to be my Lord and Savior and I accept His righteousness. I will make the choice to repent of my sinful past life." Now I know because I made the most important decision of my life; because I chose to make that decision, I get to live hallelujah days (the nine good fruits of the Spirit) forevermore.

I hope each of you makes the decision to allow Jesus to come into your life and transform you as He has transformed me forever and ever, amen. Trust me, it is the same for each and every person who will make the decision to invite Father God's only begotten Son to come into your heart and create in you a new heart as spoken about in Psalm 51:10 when King David asked God, *"Create in me a clean heart, O God, and renew a right spirit within me."* (KJV) I did this many years ago, and I now have a clean heart and right spirit within me. I have discovered to live for Christ and to "die to self" daily is more fun, and as it says in Romans 8:1, *"There is therefore now no condemnation to those who are in Christ Jesus, who do not walk according to the flesh, but according to the Spirit."* Father God Almighty will forgive each of us if we are willing to ask Jesus into our life; He then abides with you and it states in Hebrews 13:5, *"I will never leave you nor forsake you."* The Bible says in Hebrews 6:18, *"It is impossible for God to lie ...,"* so therefore I do believe every word written and divinely inspired in the Bible, which I believe is written for our benefit. Believing the Bible and claiming the promises of God, without doubt, has brought blessings galore upon me and my household. I have found if I do not doubt what God has said in the Bible, I will receive what I have prayed for; this is written in James 1:6–8, Matthew 18:19–21, Mathew 21:21–22, Mark 11:23–24, John 14:13–14, and John 15:7–8.

James 1:6–8 says, *"But let him ask in faith, with no doubting, for he who doubts he is like a wave of the sea driven and tossed by the wind, 7 For let not that man suppose that he will receive anything from the Lord; 8 he is a double-minded man, unstable in all his ways."*

Matthew 18:19–21 says, *"Again I say to you that if two of you agree on earth concerning anything that they ask, it will be done for them by My Father in heaven, 20 For where two or three are gathered together in My name, I am there in the midst of them."*

Matthew 21:21–22 says, *"So Jesus answered and said to them, 'Assuredly, I say to you, if you have faith and do not doubt, you will not only do what was done to the fig tree, but also if you say to this mountain, 'Be removed and be cast into the sea,' it will be done. 22 And whatever things you ask in prayer, believing, you will receive.'"*

Mark 11:23–24 says, *"For assuredly, I say to you, whoever says to this mountain, 'Be removed and be cast into the sea,' and does not doubt in his heart, but believes that those things he says will be done, he will have whatever he says. 24 Therefore I say to you, whatever things you ask when you pray, believe that you receive them, and you will have them."*

John 14:13–14 says. *"And whatever you ask in My name, that I will do, that the Father may be glorified in the Son. 14 If you ask anything in My name, I will do it."*

John 15:7–8 says, *"If you abide in Me, and My words abide in you, you will ask what you desire, and it shall be done for you. 8 By this My Father is glorified, that you bear much fruit, so you will be My disciples."*

I, Candice Irene, want to *be one of His disciples and bear much fruit* for the rest of my life on this earth, as I just quoted in John 15:7–8. Amen. I discovered that because I have taken God Almighty at His word written in the Holy Bible that I most assuredly have been set free from fear, worry, condemnation, guilt, anxiety, and so much more. I have learned to quote a Scripture or two or even three, when the evil ones try to invade my heart, mind, soul, family, friends, acquaintances, and whoever I am around at the time that they try to steal, kill, or destroy my peace. If I, for a moment, start to lack peace of mind, I know the evil ones are lurking. I know I must quickly pray and say the quickest prayer I ever prayed, "Jesus, help," and immediately I feel relief! Therefore, I plan to stay Scripture equipped every single second of my life so that I can remain free and have "Jesus joy" every single day of my life. I will not give up any of the benefits that are granted to me for believing in God's only begotten Son! I have been set free by the blood of Jesus, and I repeat the verse written in John 8:36, *"Whom the Son sets free is free indeed."* I would not go back to the girl I used to be before the age of fifty if you offered me all the gold in the world; it is too brutal out there; trust me, I have "been there, done that" and I most assuredly like this transformed lifestyle much more. I am now full of wisdom, knowledge, and understanding because I study God's word and I believe what I read and hear from spiritually informed teachers/preachers. The Bible states in Romans 10:17, *"So then faith comes by hearing, and hearing by the word of God."* I have made it my number one priority to listen to knowledgeable Spirit-filled preachers and teachers daily. I like knowing Scripture, and I also like knowing that God's Holy Spirit resides in me forevermore. I am now complete in Christ and I am void-free of anything that is not from my heavenly family! I am one happy woman even when there is abundant chaos around me in this fallen world. I truly love being a new creation in Christ—transformed from the inside out!

## SAY IT, BELIEVE IT, AND YOU WILL RECEIVE IT
April 3, 2020, 4:59 a.m.

This morning I woke up and I believe the LORD wanted me to write about one's attitude. It is of the utmost importance that you tell your heart, mind, and soul how you feel. I have this list by my bedside, basically under my alarm clock. It is written as such:

I AM ESTABLISHED

I AM ANOINTED

I AM BELIEVED IN

I AM SEALED BY THE BLOOD

I AM WELL ABLE

I AM BLESSED

HALLELUJAH DAYS FOREVERMORE

I AM A CHILD OF THE MOST HIGH

I AM CANDICE IRENE/JESUS' BELOVED

Upon my retirement on January 7, 2019, I started putting affirmations on an anchored background stationery and hung them around my bedroom, my bedroom door, my refrigerator, my bathroom wall, and door. I felt led to do this as constant reminders of what God Almighty wants me to believe at all times. It has been fun and I enjoy doing it the moment I have an unction from the Holy one as written in 1 John 2:20 in the King James Version only: *"But ye have an unction from the Holy One, and ye know all things."* When I discovered this verse years ago, I was elated and have been ever since. I believe an unction from the Holy One means that you hear the still small voice of God through the Holy Spirit abiding within your heart, mind, and soul, and as the verse states: *"And ye know all things."* Wow, that excites me fervently. I am very passionate about hearing what God has to say about me so as to never let life's circumstances pull me in any way that does not line up with what God says about me.

I have also learned to live my life, according to the verse written in Philippians 4:6–8 as if God were speaking directly to me. It is written as such: *"Be anxious for nothing, but in everything by prayer and supplication, with thanksgiving, let your request be made known to God; 7 and the peace of God, which surpasses all understanding, will guard your hearts and minds through Christ Jesus. 8 Finally, brethren, whatever things are true, whatever things are noble, whatever things are just, whatever things are pure, whatever things are lovely, whatever things are of good report, if there is any virtue and if there is anything praiseworthy—meditate on these things."* I have learned to do this no matter what the situation is.

The last couple of years of my physical education teaching career Father God brought the above Scripture to my mind constantly by reminding me that if there is anything good about the day or praiseworthy, only meditate on the good and do not allow my mind to wander or be dismayed to the negative at any time! As one can imagine when you are involved in a school teaching environment for eight hours per day and over one thousand individuals present, there will be good, bad, annoying, frustrating, tedious, etc. However, I learned to do what Philippians 4:6–8 taught me to do. Amen! My teaching job became fun and rewarding due to this frame of mind. As a matter of fact, I even had a very hard time making the decision to retire after thirty-seven years of teaching physical education in the Hillsborough County School System, but I did because I felt God was leading me into a brand-new senior citizen's part of my life. I have now been retired for a year and two months. God is leading me and teaching me how to live a good life as a retiree; He even directed me to write my sixth published book titled *Hallelujah Days*. It is a book about living a Galatians 5:22–23 (quoted earlier) lifestyle no matter what. I have made the deliberate choice to do this and I feel blessed indeed for doing what I feel my Father God has led me to do!

It is now 6:33 a.m. and I am going to stop typing for a few minutes and get on my knees, thanking God for my life. It is now 6:37 a.m. and without fail every single time, I am blessed enough to notice 6:33 a.m. or 6:33 p.m. The Scripture that is written in Matthew 6:33 comes to mind: *"But seek first the kingdom of God and His righteousness, and all these things shall be added to you."* Again, the word "all" appears in the verse as it did in 1 John 2:20 Beloved's "all" does mean every single thing. So, by knowing these verses, I believe God when it states all that I will ever need will be provided for me by Jehovah Jireh, meaning God our provider. God Almighty is truly an amazing Creator and Father to all who are willing to get to know Him personally as a Father as I have done. It is fun and by knowing my heavenly family very intimately, I am complete and lacking absolutely nothing. As a matter of fact, I am overflowing in many things. After typing and reading this last sentence I remembered a

Scripture verse written in the Bible by Jesus' brother James that says *"My brethren, count it all joy when you fall into various trails. 3 knowing that the test of your faith produces patience. 4 But let patience have its perfect work, that you may be perfect and complete, lacking nothing."* (James 1:2–4) That is surely a valuable verse to know and  because I believe every word written I now understand that is why I am *lacking for nothing.* Amen and Hallelujah to that knowledge. Blessed indeed are we who believe and understand what is written in the Holy Bible— God's autobiography divinely inspired for our benefit. God is so good and now it is 6:48 a.m. and I am going to stop writing for this day and go and enjoy my first cup of coffee, sitting quietly with my Father God. It is going to be a very good Friday for me!

# DELIVERED FROM THE EVIL ONE
Amen and Hallelujah
April 4, 2020, 7:04 a.m.

What a feeling of joy to know that I am delivered from the evil one as it is written in several verses of the Bible such as 1 John 4:4, Galatians 5:1, James 4:7, Psalm 32:4, Psalm 34:4, Psalm 34:17, Psalm 107:6, Isaiah 43:18–19, 1 John 5:4–5, 1 Peter 5:8–9, 2 Corinthians 10:3–4, 2 Samuel 22:2–3, John 10:9–11, 1 Corinthians 15:55–58, James 5:13–16, Romans 6:14–19, Ephesians 6:10–18, Romans 8:1–10, and Psalm 91:1–16. My favorite quote of deliverance from the evil one in these days of worldwide chaos due to the evil of the COVID-19 pandemic is Psalm 91:1–16.

*Safety of Abiding in the Presence of God*

Psalm 91:1–16 says, *"He who dwells in the secret place of the Most High shall abide under the shadow of the Almighty. 2 I will say of the LORD, 'He is my refuge and my fortress; My God, in Him I will trust.' 3 Surely He shall deliver you from the snare of the fowler and from the perilous pestilence. 4 He shall cover you with His feathers, and under His wings you shall take refuge; His truth shall be your shield and buckler. 5 You shall not be afraid of the terror by night. Nor of the arrow that flies by day. 6 Nor of the pestilence that walks in darkness. Nor of the destruction that lays waste at noonday. 7 A thousand may fall at your side, and ten thousand at your right hand; but it shall not come near you. 8 Only with your eyes shall you look, and see the reward of the wicked. 9 Because you have made the LORD, who is my refuge, even the Most High, your dwelling place. 10 No evil shall befall you, nor shall any plague come near your dwelling: 11 For He shall give His angels charge over you, to keep you in all your ways. 12 In their hands they shall bear you up, lest you dash your foot against a stone. 13 You shall tread upon the lion and the cobra, the young lion and the serpent you shall trample underfoot. 14 'Because he has set His love upon Me, therefore I will deliver him; I will set him on high, because he has known My name. 15 He shall call upon Me, and I will answer him; I will be with him in trouble; I will deliver him and honor him. 16 With long life I will satisfy him, and show him My salvation.'"*

I am truly enjoying reading and studying each of these verses that explain how I am kept from the evil one especially at this hour of so much fear in the world that is most assuredly happening. As we are ordered to stay at home for a time, I find great comfort knowing that I am not alone even though I live alone. Amen. It is written in John 16:13–15 that the Spirit of truth is always with me no matter where I go or what I do: 16:13–15 says, *"However, when He, the Spirit of truth has come, He will guide you into all truth; for He will not speak on His own authority, but whatever He hears He will speak, and He will tell you things to come. 14 He will glorify Me, for He will take of what is Mine and declare it to you. 15 All things that the Father has are Mine. Therefore I said that He will take of Mine and declare it to you."* Hallelujah to what is written in those verses and because Jesus said it, I do receive it because I am a believer and follower of our Lord and Savior who gave His life as a substitute for our sinful life as written in John 3:16, *"For God so loved the world that He gave His only begotten Son, that whoever believes in Him should not perish but have everlasting life."* I look forward to that day when He will return for all His believers and blessed followers. I am a believer and I enjoy following Jesus wheresoever *the Holy Spirit of truth* leads me. I must add that even though the world is in complete and total chaos over this virus, I am at peace. For Jesus Christ is also called the *"Prince of Peace,"* I receive His peace daily because I asked Him to be my Lord and my Savior. Blessed indeed am I because I receive what He laid His life down on Calvary, nearly two thousand years ago, for me, and for you, if you are willing to believe as I have chosen to do. When I accepted God's only begotten Son into my life, I wrote and learned what that truly meant and I gave details of my revelations in six published journey books, and since I did that dedicated labor of love, I have been blessed abundantly in wisdom, knowledge, and understanding. I have been rescued from the evil ones of this world. Hallelujah! What a heavenly family we have been blessed with! Blessed indeed are all who choose to believe what is written. It is 8:27 a.m. and I am going to sit and have a cup of coffee with the Lord and hear His still small voice of love, comforting me about the safety of me and all my loved ones, and giving me continual peace of mind.

# LIBERATED
April 5, 2020, 7:51 p.m.

This evening of Palm Sunday, I feel I have been led to write on being liberated. Jesus Christ came to set us free from the bondage of sin and death. I have made it my main priority to walk with Jesus daily and hear the still small voice, promptings, and unction's of the Holy Spirit keeping me in all my ways as it is written in Proverbs 3:6, *"In all your ways acknowledge Him and He shall direct your paths."*

I have learned to acknowledge the LORD and learn from the Bible who our God truly is and our Lord and Savior. And because I made that my number one priority, I in return feel like I am truly and completely liberated from the bondage of sin. I no longer walk in guilt, fear, worry, doubt, condemnation, sickness, etc. I have been set free. I read the Bible and I choose to believe all that I read and I claim the promises written, therefore I receive them. I am blessed and very grateful. Our Lord Jesus Christ did pay the highest price one can pay and that is His sinless life in exchange for our sinful life. In other words, He is our substitute and He paid our sin debt of death in full. We have, therefore, in return, been set free from paying the penalty for ourselves and loved ones. I call that liberated to the fullest. Amen.

As I wrote earlier, *Whom the Son sets free is free indeed.* My committed relationship, heartfelt love, and gratitude for what Jesus has done for each one of us who choose to believe and then commit to Him, in all our ways, is freed from the evil things as well as the evil ones of this world. It is written in 1 John 4:6, *"We are of God. He who knows God hears us; he who is not of God does not hear us. By this we know the spirit of truth and the spirit of error."* I like knowing the difference of truth and error; it makes me feel at peace; and peace of mind, to me, is the best it gets in this life. As a matter of fact, when my son was twelve years old and I was in my forties, my son asked me: "Mom, if you could have any three wishes that would come true, what would they be?" After sincere thinking on each wish, one at a time, the answer ended up being the same for all three wishes. The answer that I replied to my son was "Peace of mind." He was most definitely befuddled that all three would be the same! God Almighty and Jesus Christ through the Holy Spirit, reading, hearing, and studying of the Word daily have finally got it into my heart and mind that my wish is fulfilled. I have been granted peace of mind, and the Bible has taught me how to keep my peace in many places, but I am going to type Psalm 34. I feel it is the verse I was personally led to this Sunday evening.

Psalm 34:1–22 says, *I will bless the LORD at all times; His praise shall continually be in my mouth. 2 My soul shall make its boast in the LORD; the humble shall hear of it and be glad. 3 Oh, magnify the LORD with me, and let us exalt His name together. 4 I sought the LORD, and He heard me, and delivered me from all my fears. 5 They looked to Him and were radiant, and their faces were not ashamed. 6 This poor man cried out, and the LORD heard him, and saved him out of all his troubles. 7 The angel of the LORD encamps all around those who fear Him, and delivers them. 8 Oh, taste and see that the LORD is good; Blessed is the man who trusts in Him! 9 Oh, fear the LORD, you His saints! There is no want to those who fear Him. 10 The young lions lack and suffer hunger; But those who seek the LORD shall not lack any good thing. 11 Come, you children, listen to me; I will teach you the fear of the LORD. 12 Who is the man who desires life, and loves many days, that he may see good? 13 Keep your tongue from evil, and your lips from speaking deceit, 14 Depart from evil and do good; seek peace and pursue it. 15 The eyes of the LORD are on the righteous, and His ears are open to their cry. 16 The face of the LORD is against those who do evil, to cut off the remembrance of them from the earth. 17 The righteous cry out, and the LORD hears, and delivers them out of all their troubles. 18 The LORD is near to those who have a broken heart, and saves such as have a contrite spirit. 19 Many are the afflictions of the righteous, but the LORD delivers him out of them all. 20 He guards all his bones; not one of them is broken. 21 Evil shall slay the wicked, and those who hate the righteous shall be condemned. 22 The LORD redeems the soul of His servants, and none of those who trust in Him shall be condemned.* Not be in any condemnation for all my past careless choices and sins sure does give me complete peace and most assuredly a feeling of freedom and liberation. Amen! Typing Psalm 34 and agreeing with the verse has blessed me abundantly and reestablished my peace of mind even that much stronger, and to that blessing, I must say hallelujah!

## THANKFUL
April 6, 2020, 4:54 a.m.

I just had to quickly get out of bed and get to the computer this morning so I could type a thankful heartfelt note to our heavenly family before the rest of humanity comes awake. We are so blessed to be loved by such a patient/long-suffering Father. He is so patient with His hard-headed, hard-hearted children. Upon looking back, I can remember my ignorance and behavior of the things I partook in previously. I too had to suffer a trial and tribulation that only God Almighty could have rescued me and my son from.

I will never forget the afternoon when I got home from trying to convince my son that I was working in his best interest, but we had had a complete difference of understanding. One afternoon, in particular, when my son thought I was not there to help him; however, I was. So, when I arrived home from being at my son's home and unable to convince him of my sincerity, I started talking to God about the situation and clearly, in my heart, I felt my Father God saying, "Candice, now you know how I feel." I said back, "Oh God, I do." I knew how earnestly I was only wanting the very best for my son and then I knew our Father God Almighty, at all times, only wants the very best for each and every one of us for we are His beloved children too. Father God Almighty allowed His Son Jesus to be born as a baby and then live a life here on earth with us for thirty-three years and then He was rejected by His own people, suffered extreme agonizing pain, and then finally he was crucified on a cross so that He could reconcile us to our Father God with His sinless bloodshed on our behalf. Jesus is quite a man that He would do that just for us. His love is so vast and so merciful. When I think of how long-suffering our heavenly family truly is, I find myself this Monday morning just wanting to thank Them for Their extended goodness, mercy, grace, and endless love. I am so looking forward to the day when we who have fixed our hearts to believe what is written in the Bible—which is God Almighty's holy divinely inspired book of love and instructions of how to get to know Them personally and intimately— bow down and say, "Holy, holy, holy is our God of love, goodness, mercy, and abounding grace." It is explained in the Bible in the book of Corinthians that one day, on "that day," we will be with our heavenly family; that God Almighty will bring us into Himself, where we will no longer experience suffering, sadness, pain, and death. O what a day that will be, as it is written in 1 Corinthians 15:50–58, as our final victory (KJV): *"Now this I say, brethren that flesh and blood cannot inherit the kingdom of God neither doth corruption inherit incorruption. 51 Behold, I shew you a mystery; We shall not all sleep, but we shall all be changed, 52 in a moment, in the twinkling of an eye, at the last trump: for the trumpet shall sound, and the dead shall be raised incorruptible, and we shall be changed. 53 For this corruptible must put on incorruption, and this mortal must put on immortality. 54 so when this corruptible shall have put on incorruption, and this mortal shall have put on immortality, then shall be brought to pass the saying that is written, Death is swallowed up in victory. 55 O death, where is thy sting? O grave, where is thy victory? 56 The sting of death is sin; and the strength of sin is the law. 57 But thanks be to God, which giveth us the victory through our Lord Jesus Christ. 58 Therefore, my beloved brethren, be ye steadfast, unmovable, always abounding in the work of the Lord, forasmuch as ye know that your labour is not in vain in the Lord."*

Paul, who wrote Corinthians, sure was steadfast in abounding in the work of the Lord. I want to do that as well for the rest of my life out of gratitude and love for all that the Lord Jesus Christ has accomplished for us by His death, burial, and resurrection almost two thousand years ago so we could be reconciled to our Father God Almighty who art in heaven. What an amazing God we serve, and I am grateful I get this awareness and knowledge of who we should choose to walk with and follow His earthly example daily. I want myself and all my beloveds to be with me to see Him face-to-face on "that day" when He calls us unto Himself. I pray in the name of Jesus that I do all I can do and say to help my family, friends, acquaintances, and God-given people connections learn how to receive this victory over the sting of death. O what a day that will be, but until then I pray that all people come to know who our Lord and Savior truly is and why He gave His life as a substitute for each of us. Again I do pray this prayer in Jesus' mighty powerful name, amen.

One more note on thankfulness! I am grateful that the LORD our God has so graciously and lovingly brought me out of the darkness and allowed me to go through a complete transformation as written in 2 Corinthians 5:17, *"Therefore, if anyone is in Christ, he is a new creation: old things are passed away; behold, all things have become new."* I asked for this transformation, in prayer, when I saw this particular verse in the Bible and then I allowed a true *"new creation transformation"* to take place mentally and emotionally. I also believe because of His love, goodness, mercy, and grace, my family, as well, has truly experienced a true heart-and-mind transformation. I know that none of us would go back to the carnal/worldly way of thinking again because of the knowledge of what our Lord and Savior has done so that we could be with all of our loved ones in the *Kingdom to come on earth as it is in heaven.* Whenever my family members get together for any occasion, we join hands before dinner and pray the LORD'S prayer written in Matthew 6:9–13, *"Our Father which art in heaven, Hallowed be thy name. 10 Thy kingdom come. Thy will be done in earth, as it is in heaven. 11 Give us this day our daily bread. 12 And forgive us our debts, (trespasses) as we forgive (those who trespass against us) our debtors. 13 And lead us not into temptation, but deliver us from evil; For thine is the kingdom, and the power, and the glory, forever. Amen."* We are a family desiring to do our LORD'S will on this present-day earth and we are a fully believing family that if it is written in His Holy Word titled "The Bible," then it is true and for that, I am truly thankful!

# BE BOLD FOR GOD IS ON THE THRONE
April 7, 2020, 4:41 a.m.

I do have a feeling of boldness this morning for I know God is on the throne. The verse that our God put in my heart upon my wake-up from a very good night's sleep is from Romans 8:28–31 and what the devil means for harm in this life God Almighty will turn it around and it will work out for our good for He is the great "I AM." Romans 8:28–31 says, *"And we know that all things work together for good to those who love God, to those who are the called according to His purpose. 29 For whom He foreknew, He also predestined to be conformed to the image of His Son, that He might be the firstborn among many brethren. 30 Moreover whom He predestined, these He also called whom He called, these He also justified and whom He justified, these He also glorified."* What a phenomenal God we have watching over the entire universe, which He and the Word created as written in the very first verse of His Holy Bible in Genesis 1:1, and then according to Google, there are thirty-two Bible verses about the creation of the earth. I am going to have quite an exciting day looking up, quoting some of them, and reading each one of the Googled listed creation verses on this first Tuesday of April 2020.

These are some of the Bible verses about the creation of the earth:

*"In the beginning God created the heavens and the earth. 2 The earth was without form, and void; and darkness was on the face of the deep, And the Spirit of God was hovering over the face of the waters."* (Gen. 1:1–2)

*"Then God blessed the seventh day and sanctified it, because in it He rested from all His work which God had created and made. 4 This is the history of the heavens and the earth when they were created, in the day that the LORD God made the earth and the heavens."* (Gen. 2:3)

*"Where were you when I laid the foundations of the earth? Tell Me, if you have understanding. 5 Who determined its measurements? Surely you know! Or who stretched the line upon it? 6 To what were its foundations fastened? Or who laid its cornerstone, 7 when the morning stars sang together, and all the sons of God shouted for joy?"* (Job 38:4–7)

*"By the word of the LORD heavens were made, and all the host of them by the breath of His mouth."* (Ps. 33:6)

*"Lord, You have been our dwelling place in all generations. 2 Before the mountains were brought forth, or ever You had formed the earth and the world, even from everlasting to everlasting, You are God."* (Ps. 90:1–2)

*"This is the day the LORD has made; we will rejoice and be glad in it."* (Ps. 118:24)

*"I will lift up my eyes to the hills—from whence comes my help? 2 My help comes from the LORD, who made heaven and earth."* (Ps. 121:1–2)

*"Our help is in the name of the LORD, who made heaven and earth."* (Ps. 124:8)

*"Have you not known? Have you not heard? The everlasting God, the LORD, The Creator of the ends of the earth, neither faints nor is weary. His understanding is unsearchable."* (Isa. 40:28)

*"Woe to him who strives with his Maker! Let the potsherd strive with the potsherds of the earth! Shall the clay say to him who forms it, 'What are you making?' Or shall your handiwork say, 'He has no hands'? 10 Woe to him who says to his father,*

*'What are you begetting?' Or to the woman, "What have you brought forth?' 11 Thus says the LORD, the Holy One of Israel, and his Maker; 'Ask Me of things to come concerning My son; and concerning the work of My hands, you command Me. 12 I have made the earth, and created man on it. I—My hands— stretched out the heavens, and all their host I have commanded. 13 I have raised him up in righteousness, and I will direct all his ways; He shall build My city and let My exiles go free, not for price nor reward," says the LORD of hosts."* (Isa. 45:9–13)

*"Ah Lord God! Behold, You have made the heavens and the earth by Your great power and outstretched arm. There is nothing too hard for You."* (Jer. 32:17)

*"For every house is built by someone, but He who built all things is God."* (Heb. 3:4)

I will end this Google search of Scriptures with what is written in the last book of His Holy Bible, written in Revelations 5:13, *"Then I heard every creature in heaven and on earth and under the earth and on the sea, and all that is in them, saying: 'To Him who sits on the throne and to the Lamb be praise and honor and glory and power; for ever and ever!'"* It is closed with an exclamation point as our hearts should be exclaiming to the whole world and anyone or any created creature in it who thinks they can put anything over on our Father God Almighty, Our Lord and Savior, and the powerful Holy Spirit of the great I AM. O my, I do believe what's coming up soon is going to be more than the human mind can even fathom, and I am thrilled, to say the least!

I feel a sense of peace in my inner being that surpasses understanding as written in Philippians 4:7, *"And the peace of God which surpasses all understanding will guard your hearts and minds through Christ Jesus."* So when you have the great I AM and His only begotten Son, our Redeemer sitting on the right-hand side of His Father and the powerful Holy Spirit filling each and every believer with the Holy Spirit, I can feel a shaking coming upon this earth like the world has never seen before! I must admit I am excited with expectancy as I have not felt before. I also get a great sense of peace by reading and believing John 10:28–30, which says, *"I give them eternal life, and they shall never perish; no one will snatch them out of my hand. 29 My Father, who has given them to me, is greater than all; no one can snatch them out of my Father's hand. 30 I and the Father are one."* God is turning all things around, and we will see His glory in the world and all of His creation, amen!

## GOD ALMIGHTY HAS THE WHOLE
## WORLD IN THE PALM OF HIS HANDS
April 8, 2020, 2:57 a.m.

I just woke up, but I plan to go back to bed for a while after I write this inspiration. I know that our Father God has the whole wide world in the palm of His hands. I also know that if we will keep our minds on Him, we will have no worries or fears because the Bible tells us so. I wish the whole human race would believe in our heavenly family and feel the peace I feel even in the chaos of the COVID-19 virus.

The reason I have peace of mind is because I have learned to have faith and I do agree with Romans 10:17, which says, *"So then faith comes by hearing, and hearing by the word of God."* Beloveds, I implore each of you to watch and listen to Christian television such as CTN/WCLF, TBN, Daystar, Word Network, etc. I have heard many great preachers and teachers talk about what the Bible says on these particular networks. I know it is important to be aware of what is going on in the world and do take all necessary precautions, but to just stay glued to the news all day long without any mixture of Christian news, I truly believe, will cause fear, worry, and stress. Friends, those negative emotions evoked are not from God Almighty but from His clever adversary. It says in 2 Timothy 1:7, *"For God has not given us a spirit of fear, but of love, but of power, and of a sound mind."* I know the difference because I had to learn how to take every negative thought captive and disarm every spirit of fear the hard way and that, my friends, is why I keep my mind on the things that come from above and not the things of this world. Last, but not least, watch Christian movies written by true Christian producers that promote the truth of what is written in God's Holy Word.

Beloveds, if you will do all you can to gain knowledge of how our God truly loves you and me, you too can live the good fruits of the Spirit of God day in and day out like I do. I wrote a book titled *Hallelujah Days*. It is a book explaining how God taught me how to live in what He says and not what false news media and carnal believers proclaim. Our heavenly family wants us to live a Galatians 5:22–23 lifestyle even in this fallen world and that is *"Love, joy, peace, longsuffering, kindness, goodness, faithfulness, 23 gentleness, self-control. Against such, there is no law."*

God cannot lie! If it is allowed to be written in the Bible and we claim it, then it shall be ours, if we have faith enough to believe what is written in Mark 11:24, which says, *"Therefore I say to you, whatever things you ask when you pray believe that you receive them, and you will have them."* Also if God Almighty speaks His Word, it cannot come back to Him void; it even says this in Isaiah 55:11–13, *"So shall My word be that goes forth from My mouth; it shall not return to Me void, but it shall accomplish what I please, and it shall prosper in the thing for which I sent it. 12 'For you shall go out with joy, and be led out with peace; the mountains and the hills shall break forth into singing before you, and all the trees of the field shall clap their hands. 13 Instead of the thorn shall come up the cypress tree, and instead of the brier shall come up the myrtle tree; and it shall be to the LORD for a name, for an everlasting sign that shall not be cut off.'"* Hallelujah! This is saying it must be fulfilled on God's behalf. However, we must be in alignment with what our part is and that is to have faith in God and complete and total trust without wavering even when the circumstances seemed different than what the Bible says, amen.

I looked up the word "faith" in the dictionary and it is defined as (1) complete trust or confidence in someone or something, and (2) strong belief in God or in the doctrines of a religion, based on spiritual apprehension rather than proof. The scriptural definition of faith is written in Hebrews 11:1, which says, *"Now faith is the substance of things hoped for, the evidence of things not seen."* Faith is the connecting power into the spiritual realm, which links us with God and makes Him become a tangible reality to the sense perception of a person.

The Bible seems to me to be somewhat like a signed legal contract by the blood of Jesus. The Bible is God's Word for all to read, study, and understand. Listen to knowledgeable preachers and teachers, whether in person or watching on Christian television stations. Fellowshipping with other believers is certainly fun, but when one is confined to their home, hospital bed, or jail cell, etc., I find it most comforting to listen to Bible teachers and not so much media news speakers, because an unhealthy fear may be felt. Sometimes the media can give out false reports; however, the Bible says that God cannot give out false writings in His divinely inspired Holy Bible. It says in several verses that God cannot lie: Numbers 23:19, 1 Samuel 15:29, Psalm 89:35, Titus 1:2, Romans 3:4, Hebrews 6:18, etc. I have decided to quote from Hebrews 6:13:20.

## God's Infallible Purpose in Christ

*"For when God made a promise to Abraham, because He could swear by no one greater, He swore by Himself, 14 saying, 'Surely blessing I will bless you, and multiplying I will multiply you.' 15 And so, after he had patiently endured, he obtained the promise. 16 For men indeed swear by the greater, and an oath for confirmation is for them an end of all dispute. 17 Thus God,*

*determining to show more abundantly to the heirs of promise*
*the immutability of His counsel, confirmed it by an oath, 18 that*
*by two immutable things, it which it is impossible for God to*
*lie, we might have strong consolation, who have fled for refuge*
*to lay hold of the hope set before us. 19 This hope we have*
*as an anchor of the soul, both sure and steadfast, and which*
*enters the Presence behind the veil, 20 where the forerunner has*
*entered for us, even Jesus, having become High Priest forever*
*according to the order of Melchizedek"* (Heb. 6:13–20). Wow,
that was a lot to comprehend but without doubt it is written, *"It*
*is impossible for God to lie."*

I really enjoyed writing this little love book written for my
benefit and then, of course, anyone that I can possibly share it
with. I pray one day that a movie will be produced on all of
my seven journey books so others can learn how to live a life
full of peace, joy, wisdom, and understanding of who our God
Almighty and our Lord and Savior Jesus Christ truly are as I
have! I want others to come to understand how God and Jesus
love us so much that one day soon They want us to come and
celebrate the believer's gift of eternal life with Them, where
we will be with our Holy Family and believing loved ones
forevermore, amen!

As I close out this writing for today, I close out knowing that
God Almighty, the Creator of heaven and earth, has everything
in the palm of His hands. I have written about His Majesty on
these pages. I did it for my reassurance and I hope you have
discovered through my writing how to read, study, and believe
what is written so you too can live a life with complete peace
of mind and free from the pandemics and chaos in this world!
Before I close out for this precious day, I want to quote from
Jeremiah 3:33, *"Call to Me, and I will answer you, and show*
*you great and mighty things, which you do not know."* I relate

to that passage of Scripture to having God's personal phone number, which is 333 for Father, Son, and Holy Spirit. And as the message says, *"Call to Me, and I will answer you."* Beloved, if by chance you happen to wake up at 2:57 a.m. or 5:00 a.m. or midnight, it will not matter what time it is that you wake up and call Him. He is always there for you, always happy to spend time with you because you are His beloved, and He has some amazing things that He will discuss with you for as long as you want. He is always excited to hear from you; I know this as a fact because I do it all the time, whether it is morning, noon, or night, or even the middle of the night!

Here is my final prayer in closing. "Dearest Father God and Lord Jesus, I come to you with a humble heart and a grateful attitude. I pray for Your peace to be bestowed on each of my readers and upon the whole wide world. My hope is in knowing that when the time is exactly right, You will return for all who did not reject the truth written about You in the Bible, as it is written in John 3:16 and You have proven over and over again.

"Father God, and Lord Jesus, please help all of us know that You are the great I AM and You have the whole wide world in the palm of Your hands, and one day soon we will see you face-to-face. But until "that day," help us know we just need to keep the faith in what You have allowed to be written in Your Holy Bible. It is the beginning, the middle, and the conclusion for all believers, for it is written. And one day we will be in the originally intended paradise before the fall of man almost six thousand years ago. You will make a new heaven and new earth as it is written in Revelation 21:1–4, *"Now I saw a new heaven and a new earth, for the first heaven and the first earth had passed away. Also there was no more sea. 2 Then I, John, saw the holy city, New Jerusalem, coming down out of heaven from God, prepared as a bride adorned for her husband. 3 And I heard a loud voice from heaven saying, 'Behold, the tabernacle of God is with men, and He will dwell with them, and they shall be His people. God Himself will be with them and be their God. 4 And God will wipe away every tear from their eyes; there shall be no more death, nor sorrow, nor crying. There shall be no more pain, for the former things have passed away."*

So, I pray this prayer in Jesus' precious, powerful name that all will come to know You as their Father and You Lord Jesus as their Lord and Savior, who paid the price in full for us to be reconciled to Your Father and Our Father. I pray that we all get in a committed everlasting relationship with the greatest heavenly family team in all the universe. Amen.

## GOD KEEPS ME FORTIFIED
April 9, 2020, 6:33 a.m.

God Almighty continues to amaze me every day of my life. It is 6:33 a.m. and just before this time Father God's Holy Spirit walked with me through my home and reminded me of how my Abba Father God is always with me and keeps my mind focused on Him. Abba is an Aramaic word that is used as a personal intimate relationship with God, our Father, kind of how we use the term "daddy." I have several Scriptures with the dates on each one taped to my walls. At different times and different situations, the Holy Spirit keeps me grounded and fortified through the postings according to my need. He gives me a particular Bible Scripture that calms, strengthens, or brings an awareness to mind. I am grateful for the way He works with me daily. I need Him and I am glad He is always with me. I am grateful beyond words. Father God is never without just the right words, at just the right moment. He always uses Bible verses to speak to me. His messages are always in alignment with Bible Scriptures. I must add it is not audibly; it is always through an unction, prompting, or just an inner-spirit knowing. The knowing is kind of the same as understanding that your heart is pumping blood throughout your body to sustain life, but at the same time you cannot hear the pumping or even feel the heart beating, but you know it is doing its function efficiently or you would die. God's Holy Spirit's voice is usually silent for me, yet very powerful within, amen!

I have, throughout the walls of my home, Scriptures and affirmations posted somewhere that they are easy to read—whether it is in the living room, bathroom, hallway, refrigerator, or my bedroom. I must say each time I read one of these postings, it strengthens me immensely and delights my soul. By having these Scripture postings in my home, I have discovered at different times of need, just reading one of the posted affirmations, which were Holy Spirit inspired, help to fortify me. They also reaffirm His Holy Word and they keep me grounded to walk by faith each day, no matter what may occur or be on the horizon. For each day is a new day, as it is written in Psalm 118:24, *"This is the day the LORD has made; we will rejoice and be glad it."* I always choose to rejoice for I know His Holy Spirit is with me and will never leave me nor forsake me (Heb. 13:5). I am going to write from Matthew 6:33 because Father God brought me to the typewriter at 6:33 a.m. and I know that was not by accident or coincidence because I believe that particular Scripture is a fundamental one for living in God's will daily. *"But seek first the kingdom of God and His righteousness, and all these things shall be added to you."* This Scripture is God's intended will for all of us. It is written that if we will seek, above all else, His heavenly kingdom and His righteousness, then we will be living in His will and His provisions. The Scriptures just before Matthew 6:33 is where God explains that there is no need to worry because He is aware of our daily needs. Matthew 6:31–34 says. *"Therefore do not worry, saying, 'What shall we eat?' or 'What shall we drink?' or 'What shall we wear?' 32 'For after all these things, the Gentiles seek. For your heavenly Father knows that you need all these things. 33 But seek first the kingdom of God and His righteousness, and all these things shall be added to you.' 34 'Therefore do not worry about tomorrow, for tomorrow will worry about its own things, sufficient for the day is its own trouble."* Our Father God has the whole world taken care of if we will just learn to have faith!

God has awakened me to this way of life and I would not change anything because I know Father God and my Savior has all my needs taken care of! Such a good, good Provider, Father, Savior, Friend that I have in Them and so do you, for He loves us all the same, because He is love!

# IN THESE LAST DAYS
## GOD'S WILL & PURPOSE WILL PREVAIL
November 26, 2019, 6:14 a.m. revised for April 10, 2020

It is written in God's Holy Word that each of us is being implored by Christ to be reconciled to our Father God, creator of heaven and earth. 2 Corinthians 5:20 says, *"Now then, we are ambassadors for Christ, as though God were pleading through us: we implore you on Christ's behalf, be reconciled to God."* This is what Jesus Christ, the only begotten Son of God Almighty, accomplished for each of us as it is written in John 3:16–21, which says, *"For God so loved the world that He gave His only begotten Son that whoever believes in Him should not perish but have everlasting life. 17 For God did not send His Son into the world to condemn the world, but that the world through Him might be saved. 18 He who believes is not condemned, but he who does not believe is condemned already because he has not believed in the name of the only begotten Son of God. 19 And this is the condemnation, that the light has come into the world, and men loved darkness rather than light because their deeds were evil. 20 For everyone practicing evil hates the light and does not come to the light, lest his deeds should be exposed. 21 But he who does the truth comes to the light, that his deeds may be clearly seen, that they have been done in God."*

Trust me, loved ones, it is God's heart's desire that each of us be reconciled to our heavenly family and forgive all that have wronged us or that we have wronged. It is His will that each of us learn how to have a forgiving heart, no matter what! All of us fall short of always doing the right thing; it is impossible to be perfect in this fallen world, no matter how much you would strive to be. We have to make the choice to be seen through the righteousness of God's begotten Son. We must let Jesus be our substitute teacher, example, Lord, and Savior or we will perish and pay our own sin debt in full. It is written in Romans 6:23, *"For the wages of sin is death; but the gift of God is eternal life through Jesus Christ our Lord."* The Bible is written for our knowledge. If you reject what is written, you will be separated from God Almighty forever and ever!

I felt the LORD spoke these words of wisdom to me in my last year of teaching: "Candice, if you will do Philippines 4:6–7 for the rest of your life, you will have success and be at peace each and every day of your life." It says, *'Be anxious for nothing, but in everything by prayer and supplication, with thanksgiving, let your requests be made known to God; 7 and the peace of God, which surpasses all understanding, will guard your hearts and minds through Christ Jesus.'"* From that message I began to thank God even before the prayer was made manifest and, trust me, I do believe every single prayer I pray will be answered in the best way that will be good for me. God placed in my heart that when it is a prayer between He and I, it can be answered as fast as a lightning bolt, which is a hallelujah moment for me. God also placed in my heart that on some of my prayers, I must have patience and unwavering faith for sometimes it takes a lot of persuasion for some of my stubborn beloveds to understand our Heavenly Father's will for each person that He so lovingly allowed into my life. Now the next verse of Philippians 4:8 titled in the NKJV of the Bible is this: Meditate on These Things. *"Finally, brethren, whatever things are true, whatever things are noble, whatever things are just, whatever things are pure, whatever things are lovely, whatever things are of good report, if there is any virtue and if there is anything praiseworthy—meditate on these things.* I felt Father God put this on my heart: "Candice, if you will follow Philippians 4:8 every single situation, occurrence, circumstance, person, place, or thing, you will live a life filled with the good fruits of the Spirit written about in Galatians 5:22–23 and you will not open the door to my evil adversary named Satan, which means deceiver and accuser of the brethren. Nor will you open the door to any of his demonic co-workers." I understood at that moment that every single situation in life can be seen as positive rather than negative—even death. Of course, death is the worst as seen by some, but when my son said, "Mom, please don't cry and be so sad you will see Grandma [my mother] again. She is on vacation." My son let me know that because of the life she lived as a believer in our Lord and Savior, she would be raised from the dead as promised in 1 Corinthians 15:51–53 (KJV), *"Behold, I shew you a mystery; We shall not all sleep, but we shall all be changed, 52 in a moment, in the twinkling of an eye, at the last trump: for the trumpet shall sound, and the dead shall be raised incorruptible, and we shall be changed. 53 For this corruption, and this mortal must put on immortality.* I also like how 1 Corinthians 15:58 says, "Be steadfast in always abounding in the word of the Lord." *58 Therefore, my beloved brethren, be ye steadfast, unmovable, always abounding in the work of the Lord, forasmuch as ye know that your labour is not in vain in the Lord."* Those above passages of Scripture bring great comfort and peace to my heart. I plan to only meditate on the good things promised by our Father God for the rest of my life because I know our Father God has only good things in store for all who labor in love for our Lord and Savior.

I wrote my sixth journey book and titled it *Hallelujah Days* because our Heavenly Father revealed to me how to live in this fallen world as a woman full of anticipation! I plan to live a lifestyle that only includes the good fruits of the Spirit, which are listed in Galatians 5:22–23 (NIV), *"The fruit of the Spirit is love, joy, peace, forbearance, kindness, goodness, faithfulness, 23 gentleness, self-control. Against such, there is no law."* Hallelujah days ahead for all who choose to have faith in the Word of God!

I am so grateful that I listen to great teachers, preachers, etc. that teach what is written in the Bible. I have learned so much by listening to the television networks that have so many amazing studiers of what is written in the Bible and then take the time to reveal it to us so that we will have accurate knowledge of the written word and Hosea 4:6 will not happen to us: *"My people are destroyed for lack of knowledge. Because you have rejected knowledge, I also will reject you from being priest for Me; Because you have forgotten the law of your God, I also will forget your children."* O Father God, how I thank You for saving my son Garrett and I, as well as my entire household! How grateful indeed for Your goodness, mercy, and grace. How grateful I am that all my prayed for loved ones will be in eternity on *that day* that our Lord and Savior comes to rescue us from the evil ones and eternal damnation because of His unselfish act of love for all of us! Amen and hallelujah forevermore!

# RUN THE RACE OF FAITH
April 11, 2020, 7:30 a.m.

As I sat and enjoyed my cup of coffee with our Lord Jesus this morning, He brought many of the verses written in the Bible to mind about running the race of faith and keeping your eyes focused on Him and His finished work of the cross. He did this beautifully for the whole world because of His endless love. He knew His sinless bloodshed was the only way for all of us to ever be reconciled to our Father and meet His Father face-to-face. He even asked His Abba Father God if there was any other way for Him to save humanity without having to endure the crucifixion on the cross. This question is recorded in Matthew 26:39, Mark 14:36, Luke 22:42, John 5:30, and John 6:38. Obviously His Abba answered Him by what is written and informed Him that there was no other way, so Jesus is recorded as saying as He dropped to his knees in prayer, faced with his trepidation over the suffering he would have to endure on the cross in order to save all of humanity. It is recorded in the above Scriptures, but I am going to quote Luke 22:42–43, where Jesus is recorded as saying, *"Father, if it is Your will, take this cup away from Me, nevertheless not My will, but Yours be done.' 43 Then an angel appeared to Him from heaven, strengthening Him."* I want to be like that too, of course not to that degree of pain and suffering, but I now know and understand that whatever we must endure, our Father God is omniscient and always has our best interests in mind. We can trust and follow Christ's example and submit all our concerns to our Heavenly Father's hands for He is the "Great I AM" and that means "I AM" can meet all of our life's needs, no matter what they are!

Wow, what an amazing heavenly family we have! We can even know from that verse that our Father God Almighty will send one of His beloved faithful angels from heaven, to strengthen us when we are about to fold under the pressures of this world!

I have lived a very good life filled with experiences that I will remember forever. I am grateful that Father God let me live through some of the experiences that could have caused death with such an attitude that was coined by my group of friends, "If in doubt, go for it." The other one we lived by was "You only live once" and that one led us to do many careless activities because we lived with a belief that life is to be lived to the fullest and if you die, at least you did it all! Reflecting back, I am grateful I did it all but more importantly than that is that I lived through it all, amen. I will never forget when I began my writing journey at the age of fifty. After my second published book titled *Reflections*, I began to grow very weary of sitting at the computer keypad typing, typing, and more typing. My mother, Ruth, was sitting on the couch correcting my printed-out pages of the next manuscript. As Ruth was an English teacher for three decades, she was correcting and editing my third book when I said, "Mom, I can't do this anymore. Look at everyone out on the river having fun." There were many boats going by enjoying waterskiing, tubing, groups in pontoon boats, fishermen, and etc. I live on the Alafia River and look out over the river in a two-story house that the LORD led me to buy on October 16, 1997, and He helped me pay it off in 2012 from my three-decade teaching career income. But back to the statement Mom made as I said, "Mom, I can't do this anymore. It's too much work and everybody is out on the river having fun but us." She said, "Candy, you have had a good life and it is now time for you to give back." That statement made planted a seed so deep that I have never stopped coming to the computer keypad and typing what I feel I have an unction to type. I am most grateful that Paul was a dedicated author and bondservant to Jesus through all his writings that brought us Gentiles into the knowledge of who we are now. He taught us what we should keep our eyes focused on the LORD and to run the race of faith focused on the prize, which is eternity with our Father God. He teaches us of the selfless act of Jesus shedding His sacred blood so we could be reconciled to God and become ambassadors for Jesus Christ as explained and written in 1 Corinthians 5:20 (already recorded in this book). Oh, what a loyal Son he was and still is for *"He has risen,"* and we "the people" get to celebrate his resurrection day tomorrow on April 12, 2020. Amen and hallelujah forevermore.

I am thankful that my mother endured with me on editing, correcting, and encouraging me to write day after day and spending time with her getting to know our Lord and Savior. I am grateful for Mom and learning from her how to be devoted, dedicated, enduring, caring, and so much more. Our mother of three was most assuredly a self-sacrificing mother for us and others as well. She always set a good example to model after. I miss her so much. She died shortly after I finished my fifth book titled *My Priority.* As I was writing that book and she was editing it, she decided she wanted to live on the river with me, in my downstairs studio apartment. It was on Mother's Day and Mom said, "Candy, I want to live here and look out at this beautiful river for the rest of my life." I said, "Mom, are you sure?" She said, "Yes, I am sure." I was happy and I let my sister and brother know; then we all teamed up and packed up the stuff that she requested. Mom only wanted the essentials as she did not want all that she had accumulated in her Brandon home, that we all grew up in, to clutter her new living space. So, once she had her clothes, jewelry, armoires, her photographs, and her beautiful light-up knick-knack display cabinet with many beautiful pieces of Swarovski, wooded miniature ducks, turtles, etc., she was set. We put the house on the market and the next day it was purchased. Mom was with me for the rest of her life, which, much to all our surprise, was only two and one-half months. She died July 8, 2013. I was so sad and crying a lot and then my son said on the phone, "Mom, don't cry. You know she's on vacation and you will see her again." My son and I went on to discuss his statement a little more and then I must say from that moment on until just now, I never cried again. However, I am crying now because I am reflecting on the memory. But because Garrett, my son, was so on target of what life and death truly is because of all Jesus accomplished, I will see her again face-to-face and this time there will never be an end, amen. I am keeping my eyes fixed on that and I plan to run the race of faith until I hug my entire eternity family in our new glorified bodies as written about in 1 Corinthians 15 and 1 Thessalonians 4, where we will be without the wicked thieves who bring sorrow to this life. Jesus defeated Lucifer/Satan and personally took back the keys to life everlasting, amen and hallelujah. Soon we will all get to live without Satan and all his wicked self-centered, prideful, and jealous-co-workers because they choose to be evil, and no evil will be allowed in God Almighty's eternity home!

Grateful am I that the LORD called out my name and because of my mother's love and example, I harkened to the calling and persevered and wrote my life journey on page after page, day after day, and year after year, and now I understand who, what, where, and why there was no other way. We must all learn how to do as the Bible says in many places: die to self daily as Paul chose to do. Paul explains in the book of Galatians to the Galatian people the process of dying to self as one in which he has been "crucified with Christ." Paul basically makes it clear that he personally no longer lives for his own sake, but for Christ who now lives in him. Paul's old way of living life, with its propensity to sin and to follow the ways of the world, is now dead, however, I do not mean physically. The new Paul is basically personified in the book of Galatians as the dwelling place of Christ who lives in and through him. I now know that as the Holy Spirit dwelling within each believer of Jesus Christ. In other words, it does not mean when we "die to self" that we will become inactive or insensible, nor will we feel our physical bodies as dead. But rather dying to self means that the things of the old life are put to death, most especially the sinful ways and lifestyles we once engaged in. *"Those who belong to Christ Jesus have crucified the sinful nature with its passions and desires"* (Gal. 5:24). Where we once pursued selfish pleasures, we now pursue, with equal passion and zeal, that which pleases our Father God. My mother, Ruth Irene, taught me how to love others more than I love myself and then upon her death I no longer had her to hold on to physically, but I sure do have her words of wisdom, love, help, and treasured memories to hold on to. I am sure because of her that is why I now cling on to Jesus' life well-lived on this planet Earth because *He is the way, the truth, and the life* that will ultimately and one day soon get us out of Satan's evil ways of sickness, drug overdoses, wheelchairs, heart disease, viruses, selfishness, jealousy, murder, sex trafficking, abortions, and many other abominations. Until that day I plan to stay focused on what Jesus' life, Paul's life, and my mom's life taught me to stay focused on. I will run the race of faith and endure to the end, for the rest of my life, with passion and zeal, never regretting anything past, future, or present, just knowing that Jesus did it all for us! I will persevere and run the race of faith, keeping my eyes and emotional heart fixed and focused on my Lord and my Savior, pressing forward and not looking back with any condemnation or sadness, knowing that one day soon evil will be done away with!

Oh, what a journey! I am so thankful that I have been given the opportunity to live. I enjoy my present-day life very much on this little piece of paradise on the Alafia River. I enjoy my river view every morning in peace and quiet. Even though I live by myself, I do not feel alone. I get to enjoy and visit with my heavenly family in my heart, mind, and soul every single day. I know They always have unlimited time to share with me all my joys, memories, reflections, circumstances, concerns, etc. My heavenly family always brings to mind a Scripture that will delight and strengthen my soul for the day ahead. I most assuredly know that each day will be a "Hallelujah Day/good fruit of the Spirit day," which will surely be splendid for our Father God Almighty is indeed "The Great I AM," and He does give me all the desires of my heart as written in Psalm 37:4, *"Delight yourself also in the LORD, and He shall give you the desires of your heart."* I like how the New King James words that for *"If We Will" choose to delight ourselves in the things of the LORD and what is pleasing to Him*, He in return will give us the proper desires of our hearts too. He only wants the best for each of His beloveds and He knows what is best for each person that He allowed to live on His Creation. He is a good Father, a very good Father, and blessed indeed are each of us that will get in a loving Father-son/daughter relationship with Him. Trust me, loved ones, it doesn't get better than that on this beautiful planet Earth that He so lovingly created many years ago for your benefit and mine!

It is 11:31 a.m., Saturday, April 11, 2020, the day before Jesus' resurrection celebration. Blessed indeed are we who believe and learn how to live a blessed life of God and become sealed by His Holy Spirit until the day of redemption as explained in Ephesians 4: 25–32, *"Therefore, putting away lying, 'Let each one of you speak truth with his neighbor,' for we are members of one another, 26 'Be angry, and do not sin' do not let the sun go down on your wrath. 27 nor give place to the devil. 28 Let him who stole steal no longer, but rather let him labor, working with his hands what is good, that he may have something to give him who has need. 29 Let no corrupt word proceed out of your mouth, but what is good for necessary edification, that it may impart grace to the hearer. 30 And do not grieve the Holy Spirit of God, by whom you were sealed for the day of redemption. 31 Let all bitterness, wrath, anger, clamor, and evil speaking be put away from you, with all malice. 32 And be kind to one another, tenderhearted, forgiving one another, even as God in Christ forgave you."*

LORD, I pray in the name of Jesus that Your Holy Spirit will help each one of us do as the Scripture above says so we will not grieve Your Holy Spirit. For your love, goodness, mercy, and grace endures forever. Help us all learn how to appreciate the love that You and Jesus have for each and every one of us. Amen.

## SEALED AND REDEEMED
Because of the precious shed blood of Jesus Christ
April 12, 2020, 6:25 a.m.

In all the world or at least the United States of America, this April 12, 2020, is celebrated this Sunday by all believers of the resurrection of Jesus Christ the only begotten Son of God Almighty, Creator of the whole world, and everything that exists is because of Him. This morning I feel a boldness and freedom that outshines all the calamities put together because our Lord and Savior was raised from the grave and therefore took away the sting of death as written in 1 Corinthians 15: 57 (already quoted) and then because He gave His life by the shedding of His sinless blood, we get to live with the covenant blood promise that is written in John 3:16, *"For God so loved the world that He gave His only begotten Son, that whoever believes in Him should not perish but have everlasting life."*

That blood covenant promise written in John 3:16 covers all who will choose to believe that God will save us for all eternity with Him if we are believers in His only begotten Son, Jesus, who died on the cross for our sin. I choose to believe therefore I receive that promise, amen. If God makes a promise, claim it and it will be yours for God cannot lie. If God promised it, then He will deliver the promise. I have Googled how many verses are written on God's promises; Google listed over fifty encouraging Bible verses and Scripture quotes: I am going to pick a few of my favorites from this list that I claim on a regular basis.

*"The LORD will fight for you and you shall hold your peace."* (Exod. 14:14)

*"But those who hope on the LORD will renew their strength. They will soar on wings like eagles; they will run and not grow weary; they will walk and not be faint."* (Isa. 40:31 NIV)

*"'No weapon formed against you shall prosper, and every tongue which rises against you in judgement You shall condemn. This is the heritage of the servants of the LORD, and their righteousness is from Me,' says the LORD."* (Isa. 54:17)

*"If any of you lacks wisdom, let him ask of God, who gives to all liberally and without reproach, and it will be given to him."* (James 1:5)

*"Therefore submit to God. Resist the devil and he will flee from you."* (James 4:7)

*"And the LORD, He is the One who goes before you. He will be with you; He Will not leave you nor forsake you; do not fear nor be dismayed."* (Deuteronomy 31:8)

*"Have I not commanded you? Be strong and of good courage; do not be afraid, nor be dismayed, for the LORD your God is with you wherever you go."* (Joshua 1:9)

*"For I know the thoughts that I think, toward you, says the LORD, thoughts for peace and not of evil, to give you a future and a hope."* (Jer. 29:11)

*"The righteous cry out, and the LORD hears, and delivers them out of all their troubles."* (Psalm 34:17) I surely like seeing the word "all" in the passage and our LORD has indeed delivered me from my troubles and to that I do say, "Thank You, LORD!"

*"Bless the LORD, O my soul, and all that is with me, bless His holy name! 2 Bless the LORD, O my soul, and forget not all His benefits: who forgives all your iniquities, who heals all your diseases, 4 Who redeems your life from destruction, who crowns you with lovingkindness and tender mercies, 5 who satisfies your mouth with good thing so that your youth is renewed like the eagle's."* (Ps. 103:2–5)

Proverbs 3:5–6. I have previously quoted this verse, however, I do have it on my bathroom wall and it feeds my soul every morning and I especially like when The LORD promises that if we will put all our trust in Him, *He will direct our paths*; that is surely a reassuring promise to see and read every morning!

*"Ask, and it will be given to you; seek, and you will find; knock, and it will be opened to you. 8 For everyone who asks receives, and he who seeks finds, and to him who knocks it will be opened."* (Matthew 7:7–8)

*"So if the Son set you free, you will be free indeed."* (John 8:36 NIV)

*"And we know that all things work together for good to those who love God, to those who are the called according to His purpose."* (Romans 8:28)

*"That is you confess with your mouth the Lord Jesus and believe in your heart that God has raised Him from the dead, you will be saved. 10 For with the heart one believes unto righteousness, and with the mouth confession is made unto salvation. 11 For the Scripture says, 'Whoever believes on Him will not be put to shame.' 12 For there is no distinction between Jew and Greek, for the same Lord over all is rich to all who call upon Him. 13 For 'whoever calls on the name of the LORD shall be saved.'"* (Romans 10:9–13)

I got powered up as I read each verse and then it also came to me that the devil messed up again because I would have been getting prepared to be at church on time this Easter Sunday and would not have taken the time to come to this computer and desire to type from God's Holy Word because I would not have wanted to be late for this special celebrated day by Christians; some people only go to church on Easter and Christmas, which is all right as long as they are learning, hearing, and studying the Bible on other days. However, back to me: My celebration of the "Sacred Blood of Jesus" is every single day for me since knowing our Father God, our Lord and Savior, and experiencing the Holy Spirit dwelling within me because of the shed blood of Jesus, and my belief in that fact has become my number one passion and priority in this life. I am elated and joyful every day even if there is bad, very bad news broadcast on the television. Trust me, I do not take the ploys of the devil/Satan lightly, but at the same time I know how to "plead the Blood of Jesus" on every one of his clever ploys and I will admit I did have to learn that fact the hard way! But not anymore because I have studied the Bible day in and day out for years now, and I love to understand, comprehend, and then claim the promises written in God's Holy Word because they cannot come back void as it is written in Isaiah 55:11 (already quoted) and it is written in many places that "it is impossible for God to lie." So, with all that knowledge, wisdom, and understanding that the Holy Spirit has led me to comprehend, delights my soul, and gives me peace of mind beyond supernatural understanding, as it is written in Philippians 4:7 (already quoted). Trust me, beloveds, I do shout "Hallelujah" every day, and if you don't, believe me, you can ask my son Garrett, my sister Sandy, and my brother Andy. They are well aware of my vigor, zeal, and passion for our God and our Lord and Savior. As a matter of fact, they know when I call or see them, I am most likely going to quote at least one Scripture or two because everything that is said by people immediately turns my mind to thinking of a quote that would validate the conversation, debate, comments, etc. God has given me a unique gift of being able to quote Scripture from memory on the spot. I love it and it keeps me focused and grounded on what the LORD says, amen.

I am a retired physical education teacher and all my students at the last school I worked at, before retiring, knew if I asked the question to my class, "What is my favorite word?" they would all shout out, "Hallelujah!" It was fun being known as the "Hallelujah coach," very fun indeed. Just typing that made me miss my students and my PE coaching days. But at the same time, I am enjoying my senior citizen retirement days immensely too and it is all because I am in a committed love relationship with our Father God Almighty and our Lord and Savior Jesus Christ Almighty, living life with them as a daughter, and a personal friend is indeed the best it gets! I know that I am sealed by the blood of Jesus and that delights my heart, mind, and soul! The enemies of God and Jesus cannot touch me because the Bible says, *"For me and my house shall serve the LORD"* (Joshua 24:2, 15). My family and I have chosen to serve the LORD and therefore we are sealed and protected by our LORD and Savior and all the holy guardian angels of the LORD. Again I will use my favorite word, hallelujah. Hallelujah is an exclamation that is defined as "God be praised" and is also an expression of rejoicing. I rejoice every day because I know my household beloveds and I are protected, rescued, set free, and sealed forevermore by the sacred blood of Jesus Christ Almighty.

I am going to end my writing and go and enjoy a cup of coffee with my heavenly family through the Holy Spirit dwelling within me and also sealed me with the Holy Spirit of God, by whom I was sealed unto the day of redemptions, and this promise of peace was written in Ephesians 4:30, *"And do not grieve the Holy Spirit of God, by whom you were sealed for the day of redemption."* It is written; therefore, it is a fact!

Blessed indeed are we who believe and get involved in a committed sharing relationship with our Father who dwells in us through His Holy Spirit the moment we accept the fact that Jesus His begotten Son lived, died, and rose from the dead for our redemption and freedom from death and hell! Amen and hallelujah! (8:03 a.m.)

## FAITH PLUS BIBLICAL KNOWLEDGE
## FIXES EVERYTHING
April 13, 2020, 7:02 a.m.

Beloveds, in all things know that faith and biblically based knowledge is the key to living life to the fullest, and faith in God and Jesus fixes everything. I tell you the truth. If you will take every concern, worry, fear, uncomfortable situation to our Father God in prayer, through the name of Jesus, and believe in your heart that what you have prayed for will come to fruition, you will be healed, helped, and fulfilled no matter what your need is, for God is the great I AM. I know this statement to be a fact because I do it whenever I feel the need to.

I know the Scriptures in the Bible to claim when I am in need. And since I know them, I also know I will receive them for if it is written in the Holy Bible that it is impossible for God to lie. It is also written that His Word will not come back void as I quoted from Isaiah 55:11 earlier in this love book. I am going to put a few more pertinent Scriptures on the final pages of this book, that I do abide in daily and that I have not included previously. I do feel they are vital to meditate on and to live by daily as armor against the enemies and evil ones in this world. I am also doing it for my well-being. I feel at times some people do have trouble accepting the already written Holy Bible as fact. In other words, we, at times, can be lacking in spiritual discerning factual knowledge and there is only one way to get it, and that is study His written Word for yourself. Revelation 22:18–19 is written as a warning to all who are choosing not to believe or accept the holy written Word of God as the infallible truth quoted in Romans 15:4 and 2 Timothy 3:16.

Revelation 22:18–19 says, *"For I testify to everyone who hears the words of the prophecy of this book: If anyone adds to these things, God will add to him the plagues that are written in this book; 19 and if anyone takes away from the words of the book of this prophecy, God shall take away his part from the Book of Life, from the holy city, and from the things which are written in this book."* That seems clear enough to me. What about you?

Romans 15:4 says *"For whatever things were written before were written for our learning, that we through the patience and comfort of the Scriptures might have hope."*

2 Timothy 3:16–17 says, *"All Scripture is given by inspiration of God, and is profitable for doctrine, for reproof, for correction, for instruction in righteousness, 17 that the man of God may be complete, thoroughly equipped for every good work"* (NKJV). I also like the way it is worded in the New International Version of the Bible (NIV): *"All Scripture is God-breathed and is useful for teaching, rebuking, correcting and training in righteousness, 17 so that the servant of God may be thoroughly equipped for every good work."* Amen. I know if I study and hear the Word of God daily, I will be *"thoroughly equipped for every good work"* for *"it is written."* Amen and hallelujah.

I know by reading and then studying the Bible, this is how Jesus handled Satan when he kept trying to tempt him to be dishonoring or disobedient to God Almighty's written Word. This is signified in Matthew 4:1–11 and Luke 4:1–15. Both Scriptures in the NKJV have been titled *"Satan Tempts Jesus."* I have decided to quote from Luke 4 for the reequipping of my heart, mind, and soul when certain people and/or the enemies of God and His righteousness try to distract me into unrighteousness or worldly thinking again. Luke 4:1–15 says, *"Then Jesus, being filled with the Holy Spirit, returned from the Jordan and was led by the Spirit into the wilderness, 2 being tempted for forty days by the devil. And in those days He ate nothing, and afterward, when they had ended, He was hungry. 3 And the devil said to Him, 'If You are the Son of God, command this stone to become bread.' 4 But Jesus answered him, saying, 'It is written, 'Man shall not live by bread alone, but by every word of God.' 5 Then the devil, taking Him up on a high mountain, showed Him all the kingdoms of the world in a moment of time. 6 And the devil said to Him, 'All this authority I will give You, and their glory; for this has been delivered to me, and I give it to whomever I wish. 7 Therefore, if You will worship before me, all will be Yours.' 8 And Jesus answered and said to him, 'Get behind Me, Satan!' For it is written, 'You shall worship the LORD your God, and Him only you shall serve.' 9 Then he brought Him to Jerusalem, set Him on the pinnacle of the temple, and said to Him, 'If You are the Son of God, throw Yourself down from here. For it is written: He shall give His angels charge over you to keep you, and, in their hands they shall bear you up, lest you dash your foot against a stone.' 12 And Jesus answered and said to him, 'It has been said, 'You shall not tempt the LORD your God!' 13 Now then the devil had ended every temptation, he departed from Him until an opportune time. 14 Then Jesus returned in the power of the Spirit to Galilee, and news of Him went out through all the surrounding region. 15 And He taught in their synagogues, being glorified by all."* Praise the LORD that He teaches us how to overcome temptations that we too face daily. I am glad I know Scripture *"written"* so I can fight off the temptations presented to me on a daily basis. Amen and hallelujah for knowledge learned and then put into practice!

The next weapon I use to fight off temptations and evil ploys is by using the power of prayer. It says in Mark 11:23–24, *"For assuredly, I say to you, whoever says to this mountain, 'Be removed and be cast into the sea; and does not doubt in his heart, but believes that those things he says will be done, he will have whatever he says. 24 Therefore I say to you, whatever things you ask when you pray, believe that you receive them, and you will have them."* Amen to that knowledge believed and practiced daily. The next prayer verse I like comprehending is written in John 14:14, *"If you ask anything in My name, I will do it."* That is Jesus speaking to John and all of us who will believe in the name of Jesus, the name above all that will stop the devil and all his co-workers immediately, for it says in Philippians 2:10–11, *"That at the name of Jesus every knee should bow, of those in heaven, and of those on earth, and of those under the earth, 11 and that every tongue should confess that Jesus Christ is Lord, to the glory of God the Father."* Therefore, all who do try to bring adversity against anyone who has complete faith in the finished work of God's only begotten Son, whom we call Jesus and pray in the name of Jesus will be rescued and even set free from the devil and his co-workers! Hallelujah! In the Hebrew language, Jesus' name is Yeshua. I like to call Him by that name too. I, most of the time, by my family and longtime friends, am known as Candy, but as I have come into my senior years of life and since I have written and published six journey books—which brought me into my new life with Christ as my head of household and knowledge of God Almighty being called Father God by me—I now, to my new friends, am often known as Candice, and to all my book readers I am known as Candice Irene. The next powerful prayer verse that I want to quote is from Matthew 18:19–20, which says, *"Again I say to you that if two of you agree on earth concerning anything that they ask, it will be done for them by My Father in heaven. 20 For where two or three are gathered together in My name, I am there in the midst of them."* I tell you the truth: That verse has kept me afloat many times over. Since I know this verse by heart, whenever I am in any situation of concern, I call a prayer partner; or if I happen to be with another believer, I immediately pray with them. However, if I am alone, I do know many numbers of prayer lines that I do infallibly trust; I also have several loved ones that I can also call and we will agree in prayer and when I do pray in faith, I then know that I have put the requested prayer in the hands of our Father God and I do not have to concern myself with the prayed for prayer again! However, if a concern or situation does come to mind again, I simply put my focus on what Mark says in Mark 11:23–24 and I will not allow the enemies of God to steal my peace, for if it is written that if I trust what I have prayed for without allowing doubt to come into my mind, I will have what I have prayed for! Amen!

I have enjoyed writing this faith-affirming love book these first thirteen days of April 2020, for truly at this particular time in all of our lives, the evil ones of this earth are truly wreaking havoc on the entire world. I heard our forty-fifth, seventy-three-year-old President Donald Trump say on television, "This is the hardest decision I have ever had to make." And trust me, I know for a fact He has made many decisions in His lifetime. However, this particular statement made by him—he was referring to the COVID-19 worldwide "genius-virus" pandemic that has plagued our world. I called for prayer this morning just for reassurance of what is happening to everybody worldwide, and as I wrote earlier, I have several prayer-line numbers that I call when I want another witness to pray with me as written in the above Scripture (Matthew 18:19–20) because sometimes you just need a prayer warrior witness to pray with you and for you! A woman name Karen answered the prayer line at 6:30 a.m. this Monday morning, the day after our Sunday of April 12, 2020, celebration of our Lord's and Savior's resurrection. This year we were not allowed to gather in the church buildings because of this worldwide epidemic that has caused several deaths and is still looming. But back to the prayer prayed for me and over me by Karen was based on Psalm 91:10–11, *"No evil shall befall you, nor shall any plague come near your dwelling; 11 for He shall give His angels charge over you, to keep you in all your ways."* That prayer prayed over me did and will armor me up for this day to face today's journey. It reminds me as well as covers me by the precious blood of our Lord and Savior Jesus, Yeshua, Christ Almighty. I hope this little love book does for you what it has done for me!

In conclusion of today's writing I want to write from Psalm 118:24, *"This is the day the LORD has made; we will rejoice and be glad in it."* I have made the choice to rejoice and live each day knowing that the LORD has the whole wide world in the palm of His hands and nothing takes Him by surprise because He is omnipresent, omniscient, and omnipotent. Our only job is to have complete faith in what is written in God's divinely inspired Holy Bible. I pray in the name of Jesus that you do have complete faith in what is written, so you too can live a life full of the good fruits of the Spirit day in and day out, which is written in Galatians 5:22–23, *"But the fruit of the Spirit is love, joy, peace, longsuffering (patience), kindness, goodness, faithfulness, 23 gentleness, self-control. Against such there is no law."* I also pray blessings galore upon you and all your family, friends, co-workers, acquaintances, and all the people that our Father God puts or allows in your path to influence you, and this I do pray in Jesus' mighty powerful name, amen.

## THE YEAR 2020 IS THE YEAR TO BE READY
### April 14, 2020

I believe this is the time for all of us to take this "forced COVID break" from normal routine as a time to get ready! Read, study, and listen to knowledge-filled teachers and preachers of the Bible. Make sure to share all you do learn with your beloveds. I know I have enjoyed taking this break from my routine. It has given me time to focus on deepening my relationship with our Father God Almighty, God's only begotten Son, and the Holy Spirit. It has given me the time to write this book. It has given me the time to reflect on all that our heavenly family does for us. It has given me the time to appreciate all that I have, my family, friends, health, and pray for those that are in need. It has also given me many Bible verses to read, study, and put into practice such as 1 Thessalonians 5:1–11. *"But concerning the times and the seasons, brethren, you have no need that I should write to you. 2 For you yourselves know perfectly that the day of the Lord so comes as a thief in the night. 3 For when they say, 'Peace and safety!' then sudden destruction comes upon them, as labor pains upon a pregnant woman. And they shall not escape. 4 But you, brethren, are not in darkness, so that this day should overtake you as a thief. 5 You are all sons of light and sons of the day. We are not of the night nor of darkness. 6 Therefore let us not sleep, as others do, but let us watch and be sober. 7 For those who sleep, sleep at night, and those who get drunk are drunk at night. 8 But let us who are of the day be sober, putting on the breastplate of faith and love, and as a helmet the hope of salvation. 9 For God did not appoint us to wrath, but to obtain salvation through our Lord Jesus Christ, 10 who died for us, that whether we wake or sleep, we should live together with Him. 11 Therefore comfort each other and edify one another, just as you also are doing."*

In my quiet time with the Lord this month of April, I sure do feel His comfort and peace. I do desire to speak and write only things that help edify one another. I pray God will help all of us comfort and edify one another spiritually during this global pandemic, and even when it is just a memory in the history books. I pray that God's peace be with you always. I pray for health and healing for all who are in need. I pray for these things in Jesus' mighty powerful name, amen.

## LOOKING TO THE AUTHOR AND
## FINISHER OF OUR FAITH
April 15, 2020

*"Therefore we also, since we are surrounded by so great a cloud of witnesses, let us lay aside every weight, and the sin which so easily ensnares us, and let us run with endurance the race that is set before us, 2 looking unto Jesus, the author and finisher of our faith, who for the joy that was set before Him endured the cross, despising the shame, and has sat down at the right hand of the throne of God."* (Hebrews 12:1–2)

*"You will keep him in perfect peace, whose mind is stayed on You, because he trusts in You. 4 Trust in the Lord forever, for in YAH, the LORD, is everlasting strength."* (Isaiah 26:3)

The LORD surely has kept my mind in perfect peace, looking unto Jesus who is the author and the finisher of our faith. Trust me, loved ones, it does not get better than that in this unique historical month of April 2020!

## TO GOD BE THE GLORY
April 16, 2020, 1:47 a.m.

The global COVID-19 pandemic, if nothing else, does give each one of us an opportunity to examine our heart, as we are commanded to stay home. I pray in the name of Jesus that each one is finding out what is most important in this life, as I have!

Matthew 6:19–21 says, *"Do not lay up for yourselves treasures on earth, where moth and rust destroy and where thieves break in and steal; 20 but lay up for yourselves treasures in heaven, where neither moth nor rust destroys and where thieves do not break in and steal. 21 For where your treasure is, there your heart will be also."*

This is giving each of us the opportunity to examine what is most important within our hearts. Are you weighed down so heavily with outside-your-home issues that you don't have time or energy to focus on Christ? The first step is to admit you need to make a change. Getting your priorities under control will help you grow closer to the Lord.

I have discovered there is absolutely no priority or issue more important to me than my relationship with the LORD and our Savior Jesus Christ. I pray at this moment that it is what is most important to you as well. I do pray this in the mighty name of Jesus Christ our Lord and Savior, amen!

If you will put God first, everything else in your life will fall into place at just the right time. Trust me, I have been living this life of putting God first since I was fifty years old, and my life is fitting into place just like a puzzle. I especially like a verse in Ephesians 2:10 (NLT) that says, *"For we are God's masterpiece. He has created us anew in Christ Jesus, so we can do the good things he planned for us long ago."* I know my life coming into complete balance is not by coincidence but instead by divine inspiration and God's guidance. God has blessed me and my household in abundance. I have no debt, no worries or concerns, and my health is as if I were still in my twenties or early thirties. I am blessed to have grown up in Florida and have a home on the Alafia River. I always enjoy watching all the boaters, paddlers, canoers, water skiers, tubers, fisherman, commercial crabbers, and wildlife of fish jumping, dolphins going by on a daily basis, and birds of all varieties constantly flying or diving for fish to eat is always entertaining, to say the least. I like it when my son and his fiancée stop in for a long stay. I always have family stopping by or at least calling to check on me. My sister often comes over so we can go on a paddleboat outing. I often take my 10-foot powerboat out for a cruise, and trust me, the list could go on and on because of the daily activities on the Alafia River.

I have discovered the activities on the river are ever-changing, but my heart for God is grounded. I enjoy coming to the computer keypad and typing the moment God impresses me with an unction to do so. I can hear His heart's desire for me when I type these pages and put my feelings from within on the page. I believe I hear God's still small voice, and it is my priority to honor Him immediately. I type so I can understand what He is trying to communicate with me. This morning I believe He is giving me an awareness of my love for enjoying and appreciating what the LORD has blessed me with. I believe He helped me realize how grateful I truly am when I take the time to thank our heavenly family by recognizing how deeply loved we all are by our Creator and heavenly family. They are full of endless love and always ready to share in our day with Their time and energy. I pray you are enjoying this time off and looking forward to what

God has in store for all of His faithful followers. I believe God will turn this COVID-19 worldwide shutdown around for our good as it is stated in Romans 8:28, *"And we know that all things work together for good to those who love God, to those who are the called according to His purpose."*

Dear God, I pray in the mighty name of Jesus that all people take this pandemic shutdown time to comprehend and realize what should be each person's priority, which, of course, is Your Kingdom to come on earth as it is in heaven. Father God, help each person realize that You are their source and not to depend on worldly sources. I hope we all learn to appreciate what You have already supplied and to be grateful for our lives, health, family, friends, and the provisions that You have made possible for each of us to enjoy. Also, to know that You will supply all our needs sufficiently and proficiently. I do pray in the most powerful name in the world, and that is Yeshua Jesus, our Lord and Savior forevermore in heaven and on earth!

Thank you, Heavenly Father, for all your goodness, mercy, grace, provisions, patience, kindness, love, joy, peace, gentleness, faithfulness, and self-control, which, of course, are the fruit of the Holy Spirit as listed in the Epistle of Galatians 5:22–23. You have taught me how to appreciate Your Holy Spirit attributes and filled my life with the good fruits of the Spirit daily. I am willing to share your never-ending love with whomever You personally bring into my path. You are my priority and I am grateful that I have learned where my heart is! I am focused on what Your heart's desire is for me and my household, which includes all my prayer-umbrella-listed names that You asked me to keep track of many years ago. God, I could write until the sun comes up on how good You have been to me and all the people I am led to pray for.

## IN EVERYTHING GIVE THANKS FOR THIS IS THE WILL OF GOD IN CHRIST JESUS
### April 17, 2020

When I read 1 Thessalonians 5:12–22, I was highly touched. *"And we urge you, brethren, to recognize those who labor among you, and are over you in the Lord and admonish you. 13 and to esteem them very highly in love for their work's sake. Be at peace among yourselves. 14 Now we exhort you, brethren, warn those who are unruly, comfort the fainthearted, uphold the weak, be patient with all. 15 See that no one renders evil for evil to anyone, but always pursue what is good both for yourselves and for all. 16 Rejoice always, 17 pray without ceasing, 18 in everything give thanks; for this is the will of God in Christ Jesus for you. 19 Do not quench the Spirit. 20 Do not despise prophecies. 21 Test all things; hold fast what is good. 22 Abstain from every form of evil."*

I surely do appreciate our Apostle Paul's steadfast fortitude in continuing to write His epistles with such thorough guidance and supernatural knowledge. To point blank tell, and explain the will of God, and *in everything give thanks in Christ Jesus.* Beloveds, if you would be willing to do the eleven listed steps above, Paul tells us we will be in the will of God. Praise the LORD, I am grateful to Paul for listing them so clearly. I am going to work diligently on trying with all my heart, mind, soul, and strength to do the above for the rest of my life.

I pray you will also have the desire to please God and live in His will today, tomorrow, and forevermore. I also pray His Holy Spirit will help each one of us achieve this goal and to help us accomplish living a thankful life from this day forward. I pray each of you will always keep in mind that even if the devil makes a troublesome situation for your harm, God will turn it around for your good if you have belief in Christ Jesus and this is written in Romans 8:28 and Romans 8:31 (these Scriptures are already quoted). I pray peace be with you always; I pray this prayer in Jesus' name. Amen.

## NEVER CONDEMN OR JUDGE
"Let all that you do be done in love"
April 18, 2020, 6:52 a.m.

On the morning of Saturday, April 18, as I was pondering something I saw posted on Facebook, I was reminded by the Holy Spirit, I am to be very careful not to judge others, but if given the opportune time, I am to teach accurate knowledge but never condemn or judge for someone's obvious lack of biblical knowledge and God's written standards. I was also brought to the Scripture in 1 Corinthians 16:14 (ESV), *"Let all that you do be done in love."* And to that refreshing reminder I say, amen.

# HARKENED TO THE LORD'S CALL
## April 19, 2020 12:12 a.m.

On the morning of April 19, the LORD woke me up. As I harkened to His call, I was wondering, what message does He want to give me this Sunday? He simply said, "If you will always be obedient and harken to my call, you and your entire household will receive blessings galore—more than you could have asked for or dreamed of."

I like getting quickly out of bed to type this message from the LORD our God. I have been blessed indeed, more than I can possibly fathom. Our heavenly family is so amazing, so amazing indeed!

## A WEALTH OF WISDOM = WOW
December 18, 2019, 6:47 a.m. revised for April 20, 2020

I truly believe with all my heart that I "get it!" By get it, I mean I truly believe I see with 2020 vision not only physically but mentally as well. I have been listening to Bible scholars, attending church, and reading the Bible for years now and self-publishing journey books for over two decades now. This morning I feel elated, grateful, blessed, knowledgeable, and full of godly wisdom on how to do it God's way and not man's way. Wow, this is a feeling of great relief and reward for my soul.

I truly believe I am seated with Christ in life. I have come to understand who, what, where, and when I became the woman I was created to be. It has not been an easy journey, but most definitely a fulfilling journey, and though I have not fully arrived at my destination of eternity, I am most confident that when our Lord and Savior does return for all who believe in the Holy Bible–written stories, I will be caught up with my beloveds in the twinkling of an eye as written about in 1 Corinthians 15. I am so excited about my journey and my destiny. I now plan to live and fulfill God's planned purpose for my life on this earth and then on "That Day," I will be with my Father God Almighty, my Lord and Savior, the host of guardian angels that went about doing the work of our Holy, Holy, Holy God Almighty, as well as all the people who died believing in the Savior of the world. Our Savior came and lived among us and allowed Himself to be crucified so that we could be redeemed, restored, and saved forevermore as written in John 3:16 (already quoted) and many other places throughout the Bible.

The Bible came alive for me, and the more I read it and listened to great teachers of the Word, I became fascinated by its contents and passionate about learning all I could about life with Christ as my example now and for all eternity. I fill complete, satisfied, happy, and content no matter what the circumstances are that I may be involved in, or that I may soon be facing because I am grounded in the Bible and what God says about me—His beloved daughter, Candice Irene.

My writing, journaling, listening, and most importantly my praying has allowed me to feel full of God's anointing oil of overflowing love. It is a feeling like no other that I have ever experienced! I am glad I cannot change a thing in my past for God has turned it all into a beautiful masterpiece of love. I now know He used every sorrow, tear, concern, worry, fear, etc. into a garden of love. He helped me grow day by day into the woman I am today. I will live the good fruits of the Spirit listed in Galatians 5:22–23 (already quoted) for the rest of my life. Wow, this is most definitely the greatest liberating day of my life because I know I am God's beloved and where I am headed forevermore. God is in control and has the whole wide world in the palm of His hand as stated in the Bible; some of the verses that state this are written in Proverbs 31, John 5:21–30, Isaiah 49:15–17, and Psalm 95:4, and when I Googled this, Google also informed me that there are 99 Bible verses about God's hand and knowing Jesus.

Beloveds, I tell you the truth, unless you get into God's written Word titled the Bible, you will be wandering around like a sheep without a shepherd. I implore you to do as I have done and turn your life over to Father God Almighty, Creator of All. I have and I will never go back to the life of letting people shepherd me because I now know the Great I Am. He is also Immanuel—God with us. He is my Life Leader, Shepherd,

Director, Keeper, etc. I am full and blessed beyond because I know the "Truth" and I have been set free and *who the Son sets free is free indeed.* This fact is written in John 8:32, which says, *"And you shall know the truth, and the truth shall make you free."* Amen and hallelujah forevermore!

# FEAR NO EVIL
April 21, 2020, 11:35 p.m.

*"For God has not given us a spirit of fear, but of power and of love and a sound mind."* (2 Timothy 1:7)

At this particular time in our history, if you are experiencing any fear whatsoever, you need to look deep within and see if you really believe John 3:16, which says, *"For God so loved the world, that He gave His only begotten Son, that whosoever believeth in Him should not perish, but have everlasting life."* God and Jesus are calling each of us unto Himself.

Now is the time to repent, call out to Jesus, and ask Him to come into your heart and reveal Himself to you. He is just waiting for you to ask Him into your life, hang out with Him, and get to know Him. I can tell you from my experience I called out to Jesus! And since I did that, my whole life has changed. I now only experience the good fruits of the Spirit, no matter what is occurring around me, even if it is the COVID-19 virus. Fear is a spirit, and it is an evil spirit that is always lurking, seeking whom he may devour; this is explained in 1 Peter 5:8, *"Be sober, be vigilant; because your adversary the devil walks about like a roaring lion, seeking whom he may devour."* For that matter, any spirit that is not of the good fruit of the Spirit listed in Galatians 5:22–23 is not a spirit from God but instead from the evil devil—he is constantly *seeking whom he may devour!*

God's Spirit within your heart, mind, and soul is *"Love, joy peace, forbearance, kindness, goodness, faithfulness, 23 gentleness, and self-control . . ."* (NIV) If you are experiencing any other spirit than the nine listed above, it is from the devil and you must take authority over all other evil spirits and cast them out of your heart, mind, and soul. God has given all Jesus believers all authority and power over the evil devil. However, you must believe in Jesus to receive this confidence and boldness or else the enemy can pick up on your disbelief and actually cause more harm. The devil is aware of your disbelief and causes stress, worry, fear, doubt, etc. But if you will find out who Jesus is and what He has accomplished for you and learn to call on the name of Jesus, beloveds, you will experience the good fruits of the Spirit, as well as what Paul, the bondservant of Jesus, has written in Ephesians 3:16–21, *"That according to the riches of his glory he may grant you to be strengthened with power through his Spirit in your inner being, 17 so that Christ may dwell in your hearts through faith—that you, being rooted and grounded in love, 18 may have strength to comprehend with all the saints what is the breadth and length and height and depth, 19 and to know the love of Christ that surpasses knowledge, that you may be filled with all the fullness of God. 20 Now to him who is able to do far more abundantly than all that we ask or think, according to the power at work within us, 21 to him be glory in the church and in Christ Jesus throughout all generations, forever and ever. Amen."* (EVS Study Bible)

Fear is not from God but just the opposite. It is an emotion that His adversary the devil survives and thrives on. If the devil can have God's people experience fear, then he can also cause God's people to doubt Him and His beloved only begotten Son Jesus. Jesus is your substitute and paid the full price of your sin debt. If you will accept Jesus as your substitute, then you can claim every single promise written in the Bible and it will come true and will not come back void. God's word cannot return to Him void as written in Isaiah 55:11, *"So shall My word be that goes forth from My mouth; it shall not return to Me void."* It is time for each and every one of us to take all authority over the evil devil and all his evil co-workers, for God has given us the authority over all evil if we will believe in the righteousness of Christ Jesus and allow Him to be our substitute for our sin debt and be our Lord and Savior. He has saved us from all the evil ones and even given us all power and authority over Satan and all his evil co-workers; this is written in Luke 10:19, *"I have given you authority to trample on snakes and scorpions and to overcome all the power of the enemy; nothing will harm you."*

Please, friends, listen to what God says in the Bible and not what the enemies of God say in the world. You do not have to live in fear, worry, anxiety, stress, disease, and all the other calamities of the devil. Please wake up to what Jesus has accomplished for you and kick the devil and all his co-workers out of your life forever and your beloved family's life too! I pray in Jesus' name you will use your God/Jesus-given authority to rebuke all demonic spirits out of your life and I pray you to do this today! Jesus did this act of love for you to become all that God created you to become. Call on him today. He will be with you immediately and never leave you nor forsake you, as written in Hebrews 13:5. I know this to be a fact, as I am thankful beyond words that God and Jesus rescued me and my son years ago from the evil ploys of Satan and his co-workers! We now live our lives filled with love, joy, peace of mind, and all the other fruits of the Spirit daily and to that, I do say to God be the glory!

## THANKFUL, CONTENT, AND AT PEACE
Fill in for April 22, 2020, 7:17 a.m.

This morning as I was enjoying a cup of coffee with the front door open to the sounds of the birds and the beautiful, relaxing view before me, I felt so thankful, content, and at peace. God is so good to us and has such a good plan for our lives.

As I was sitting, alone, with the LORD, I happened to look over and notice my posted Scripture hanging on the wall. The Scripture writing is from John 15:16, which says, *"No longer do I call you servants, for a servant does not know what his master is doing; but I have called you friends, for all things that I heard from My Father I have made known to you."* That is so amazing that our Lord Jesus would do that for us; what a gift we have from Him! I am so thankful, grateful, and most assuredly looking forward to everything He has planned for His believers and followers. And then to actually be called a friend of our Lord and Savior Jesus, that is a comfort to my heart. I love being in the safest friendship I have ever known. Jesus will be my forever lifetime friend, that is most definitely a reassuring verse. Blessed indeed are we who choose to believe!

## STAND STRONG
## BE CALM
## AND WATCH THE DELIVERANCE OF THE LORD
April 23, 2020, 12:43 a.m.

Stand strong, continue to be in faith, and watch the deliverance of the LORD like you have not experienced before. God will not be mocked. He hears all the prayers and cries of His beloveds. He stands at the door and knocks. For all those who choose to believe, you will see the salvation of the risen Lord. All who chose not to believe will wish they had. Oh God, is there is anything I can do to help? Please let me know if I can help in any way. I am willing. Please guard my tongue and help me only to say words that will edify You, and this I pray in Jesus' name amen.

Revelation 3:20 says, *"Behold, I stand at the door and knock. If anyone hears My voice and opens the door, I will come in to him and dine with him, and he with Me."* Lord, you are welcome in this home. Please come in and dine with us and help each one reading this to know how to hear your voice and your knock, and this I pray in Jesus' mighty powerful name. Amen! 1:02 a.m.

## PLEAD THE BLOOD OF JESUS
Fill in for April 24, 2020

As I sat with the LORD this morning, I started thanking Him for everything in my life. I was letting Him know how grateful I am for my son, family, health, friends, past relationships, homestead, and my retirement lifestyle. I feel so blessed at this time of my life and as I was reminiscing with the LORD, I felt the Holy Spirit brought this revelation to my mind: Teach my people to "plead the blood of Jesus." I was looking at a picture of my son, on my living room wall, when this revelation came upon me.

I want to teach people how important it is to plead the blood of Jesus over any occurrence or situation that may be happening or might be on the horizon as I can now discern quickly because of my deeply committed relationship with our Lord and Savior. His sacred blood sacrificed on the cross at Calvary years ago fixes everything, and pleading the "blood of Jesus" over anything of concern scatters the demons. They know what the blood of Jesus represents, and so do I. I pray that you also learn how powerful it is to plead the blood of protection over any and all situations that may be pressing, especially when spoken out loud!

Our holy heavenly family has every single situation in control. It may appear chaotic to us, but to God, it was already prophesized from the beginning as He is the Great I AM. He is not surprised by anything or anyone. He is all-knowing; therefore, I get to write this entire book started on April 1, 2020, with peace of mind for I have chosen to be in a committed relationship with our holy family. I am going to pray for all the people reading this page right now:

Dear Father God, I come to you with a thankful heart, anxious for nothing as it is written in Philippians 4:6–9, *"Be anxious for nothing, but in everything by prayer and supplication, with thanksgiving, let your request be made known to God 7 and the peace of God, which surpasses all understanding, will guard your hearts and minds through Christ Jesus. 8 Finally, brethren, whatever things are true, whatever things are noble, whatever things are just, whatever things are pure, whatever things are lovely, whatever things are of good report, if there is any virtue and if there is anything praiseworthy—meditate on the things. 9 The things, which you learned and received and heard and saw in me, these do and the God of peace will be with you."*

LORD, I pray for all of us to be at peace knowing what the Bible says is going to happen, in His perfect timing! You knew it all beforehand. I thank You this morning that all things are going to work together for our good. Help your people know to plead the blood over all disturbing things knowing You've got us covered. Help us hear your voice through our Holy Spirit promptings within our heart, mind, and soul. Let's walk with our heads held high knowing You are saying, "This is the way; walk in it." Let your people know in their heart You are with us and will never leave us nor forsake us as You were with Moses, Joshua, Daniel, David, Joseph, Esther, and all the other faith-filled biblical characters, for a time such as this! As our country is going through this COVID-19 satanic attack, let our people know Satan is a defeated foe and the battle has already been won. Guard our leaders' hearts. Let them know to call on what is written in Psalm 91, for it is written for our peace. Let them know in their heart and mind that your guardian angels will keep demonic attacks in alignment with what You have allowed, for it is already written in Your Holy Word, the Bible, for a time such as this.

I thank You for hearing and receiving my prayer this beautiful morning that You have provided for us this day. Help each person come to understand the sacred blood of Jesus has taken care of everything and soon all will be as You originally intended even before You formed Adam. This prayer I pray in Jesus' powerful name above all names, amen.

My second prayer for this day is this: that all will accept the finished work of the cross so lovingly accomplished and completed by our Lord and Savior. I also pray that all will come to repentance, learn the truth written in the Holy Bible, be set free from the wiles of the enemy, and be an overcomer, for the Bible does say in Revelation 3:21, *"To him who overcomes I will grant to sit with Me on My throne, as I also overcame and sat down with My Father on His throne."* This is my prayer request this day in Jesus' powerful name, amen. 8:28 a.m.

## PSALM 118:24
### April 25, 2020, 7:26 a.m.

This Saturday morning as I woke up and sat with the LORD and enjoyed a cup of coffee, I walked to my sliding glass door and looked out over the Alafia River. I noticed a few dead branches on my beach and dock. I decided to go downstairs to pick them up so I could enjoy the beauty more; then I saw a few weeds growing so I pulled them up by the roots and put them in the trash. I walked back upstairs and poured another cup of hot coffee. I began thanking the LORD for my life and all the good things He has allowed to happen in my life. I was conversing with Him, thanking Him, feeling so elated for my health, family, friends, my home, and also coming to the conclusion of this month of April 2020 writings.

The LORD brought the verse to mind that I truly love to quote, even if the day is going a bit tough. In reality, my brother Andy, whom I often go to if I need a man's point of view on a situation or happening—he always listens and then if He is not sure how to respond, he will often say, "I see"—he also says, "I think you should enjoy the day and see how the LORD works that out for you." My brother's words of wisdom years ago led me to this Scripture that has now become one of my favorites: Psalm 118:24, which says, *"This is the day the LORD has made; we will rejoice and be glad in it."*

The LORD brought that verse to my mind this morning, and memories of my life flashed before my eyes, helping me remember that our Father God does indeed have every situation and occurrence in the palm of His omniscient hands. I have learned to trust the LORD with all my heart, mind, soul, and strength, and in return, He has fulfilled my life and my family's life to fullness of love, joy, peace, and so much more. I am grateful and have made the *choice to rejoice* in the LORD every single day of my life because as it says in the Psalm quoted above, *this is the day* our Creator has made, and Jesus Christ has made it possible for us to live a life without fear. He gave His life as a substitute for our sins, which made a bridge back to living a life full of the good fruits of the Spirit every day, if we make that our choice. I am eternally grateful and look forward with great anticipation to "That Day" that we will hug Jesus and be without all the wicked evil spirits. So again, I say let's rejoice, enjoy this beautiful day and life that our God created and our Lord and Savior shed His blood on Calvary so that we could be full of all the LORD'S blessings now and for all eternity! Amen and hallelujah days, no matter what is happening in our world. God's got the whole wide world in the palms of His hands.

## KINGDOM REVELATIONS REITERATED TO ME
April 26, 2020, starting at 7:17 a.m. Sunday morning

God revealed to me that He is working a great and mighty work in me as it says in Ephesians 2:10, *"For we are His workmanship, created in Christ Jesus for good works, which God prepared beforehand that we should walk in them."* I feel like I am ready and willing to walk in all that God has prepared for me at this retirement time of my life. I feel very connected to our LORD, especially this Sunday morning of April 2020. God is reminding me of two verses, in particular, this morning. This season has unlocked many revelations for me and re-brought them to mind as we are in this COVID-19 virus pandemic period of history. God seems to be reminding me of the Scriptures that keep me focused on His plans for me. His enemy is always seeking whom he may devour as stated in 1 Peter 5:8, *"Be sober, be vigilant; because your adversary the devil walks about like a roaring lion, seeking whom he may devour."* God continually reminds me that He is with me and if I start to get concerned, He then brings Joshua 1:9 to mind. *"Have I not commanded you? Be strong and of good courage; do not be afraid, nor be dismayed, for the LORD your God is with you wherever you go."*

I know this virus is not God's doing; it is His adversary's plan to cause harm. However, as we should know, every plan the enemy conjures up, God does turn it around for our good as written in Romans 8:28, *"And we know that all things work together for good to those who love God, to those who are the called according to His purpose."* I also like knowing Romans 8:31, which says, *"What then shall we say to these things: If*

*God is for us who can be against us?"* God fills my soul with
His revelations morning, noon, and night. He keeps me fortified
against His enemies without ceasing.

I believe God is calling each of us to an awareness of His
kingdom to come. I also believe many people are longing to be
in His holy presence. They no longer desire to succumb to false
promises and illusions of false pleasures. If you will realize that
family and friends working in unity are what is truly fulfilling;
then I truly believe you will understand God's purpose and plan
for all His people.

These particular Scriptures that I will list for you are my
fortress in times of circumstances that are not within my
control. However, I have learned to pray quickly when I feel
concerned and I do use Scripture during my fervent prayers. I
have each of these verses taped to a wall in my home. They feed
my heart, mind, and soul all the time. I highly suggest that you
tape biblical quotes to a wall as I have or at least know them
and understand them so you too can have a personal hedge
of protection against the wiles of the devil. For me, reading
these posted quotes provide strength to fight God's enemies. I
personally believe God's enemies are growing in numbers daily!
I can tell the demonic enemies of God are growing in number
just from the little bit of news I do watch. I feel it is necessary
to watch some news so I can stay abreast of current-day alerts
and events.

I believe all verses from the Bible are inspired by God and
are written through a divinely inspired chosen writer. I also feel
God's divine inspiration while I am writing all of my journey
books. I believe God Almighty is downloading strength and
fuel for my soul to feast on when the enemy tries to eat me
alive through my mind or my circumstances. I use Scripture to
fight the invisible enemy of God, just like the air we all breathe

is invisible but it is real or you would be dead without air to breathe. God made the air and atmospheric pressure to sustain us for His kingdom to come soon. Satan and all his evil co-workers will not be allowed in God's loving kingdom to come; as a matter of fact, they will be thrown into "the lake of fire" and be no more! The Bible says they will be ash under our feet in Malachi 4:3, *"You shall trample the wicked, for they shall be ashes under the soles of your feet on the day that I do this,' says the LORD of hosts."* I always think of ash as a great fertilizer for new growth, the same way we use cow manure for fertilizer, as it causes all things to grow strong and healthy.

Loved ones, if you will use some of these Scriptures that I will list below as fertilizer and fuel for your soul, you will grow into the person God created you to be. You are His beloved, you are His masterpiece, you are the apple of His eye. He has His righteous right hand upon you and all your family! You must ask Him into your life and believe that God sent His only begotten Son to live as your example for thirty-three years then Jesus allowed God to have His holy blood shed on the cross at Calvary to pay your sin debt in full. This was accomplished and completed so we could all walk blameless for all the reckless choices made and may still be making. Loved ones, let Jesus be your sin sacrifice and allow His death to be your new beginning of growth that will be for now and all eternity. I did and I have never been so at peace and content filled with expectation and hope that is almost unfathomable to comprehend!

I pray at this moment that you do as I have done. Accept what the Bible says, claim the verses that best fit your circumstance, claim them as your defense against the invisible adversaries that infiltrate people. Cast them away from you, resist the negative thoughts that enter your mind, stay steadfast using Scripture, and watch your life blossom into a beauty that will be everlasting.

God, I pray their hearts will accept Your Holy Spirit's still, small, and silent voice, just like the pump of our hearts, which is indeed pumping blood without fail or we would be dead. I pray each person reading this prayer will command the evil spirits that we encounter daily to leave in the mighty powerful name of Jesus. The sinless sacrifice that has been given so we could be reconciled to our holy heavenly family forever. I pray this prayer in Jesus' name and I thank you, Father God, for hearing and answering this prayer on Sunday, April 26, 2020, at 7:51 a.m.

"Dear God, I am grateful for all that You do for all of us and how You bless us with your Holy Spirit's presence, goodness, mercy, and grace every day of our lives while we are still alive and also for our loved ones, which are resting in the grave and will arise from their sleep (death) as promised in 1 Corinthians 15:50–58 (already quoted) and 1 Thessalonians 4:16–17, *"For the Lord Himself will descend from heaven with a shout, with the voice of the archangel, and with the trumpet of God. And the dead in Christ will rise first. 17 Then we who are alive and remain shall be caught up together with them in the clouds to meet the Lord in the air. And thus, we shall always be with the Lord."* God, Your love is so vast. I pray at this moment each person reading this "thank-you prayer" receives what You have done for us and shares it with all the people they have an opportunity to chat with and come in contact with. I thank You and I praise You this day and forevermore, amen."

I am going to share some of the verses on my bathroom wall. They are my personal arsenal to fight the devil and his demonic evil spirits. The devil constantly commands his army of demons to try to steal God's people; he never ceases to try to steal, kill, and destroy God's children as written in John 10:10; they are relentless and without remorse! *"The thief does not come except to steal, and to kill, and to destroy . . ."*

God, Jesus, the Holy Spirit, and God's holy host of guardian angels could not get through to Lucifer and all the other created angels that sided with him, so they had to be cast out of God's holy heavenly kingdom. They are now demonic and are creating a needless war on earth; for the battle has already been won by the sinless crucifixion of Jesus Christ. He was the sacred final sacrifice that was lovingly given so that Satan had to give back the keys and his demonic dominion of earth. Lucifer was given full dominion of the earth by God's first created man named Adam. Adam was created by God as explained in Genesis 2:4 and 3:24 many years ago. The war is over, the battle has been won, and it is now your turn to decide which team you want to be on. If you pick the holy team of God Almighty, the Creator of heaven and earth, His only begotten Son, the Holy Spirit, and the host of guardian angels, then you too will be a victor on the winning team and no longer a victim! However, it is your choice alone, all alone. If you are over twelve years old—I believe children under twelve are still under grace; that is my belief. Which team do you choose? God has chosen each of us to be on His team, but He cannot go against your heart's desire. He has tried to send you messengers, team players, and agents of goodness, but ultimately you must choose life with Christ or death with Satan. There is absolutely no in between team. So, with all that was written, I will give you a list of the arsenal that keeps me secure while we are living on this earth waiting for His kingdom to come.

God has given me many revelations and is continuing to do so. He is letting me know He is with me and will never leave me nor forsake me. He has assured me through Scripture that He will fight every single fear, worry, or concern that comes upon me from the enemy. The enemy is always seeking God's people without ceasing! Here is a list of my bathroom wall postings that

I know by heart. I will post them in the order they are dated as that is the time of day or evening that God filled my inner spirit with His Holy Spirit's fortifying messages.

The first three were posted on my bathroom mirror in 2011:

*"However, when He, the Spirit of truth has come, He will guide you into all truth; for He will not speak on His own authority, but whatever He hears He will speak; and He will tell you things to come."* (John 16:13)

*"These things I have spoken to you, that in Me you may have peace. In the world you will have tribulation; but be of good cheer, I have overcome the world."* (John 16:33)

The Gift of Peace: *"These things I have spoken to you while being present with you. 26 'But the Helper, the Holy Spirit, whom the Father will send in My name, He will teach you all things, and brings to your remembrance all things that I said to you. 27 Peace I leave with you, my peace I give to you; not as the world gives do I give to you. Let not your heart be troubled, neither let it be afraid."* (John 14: 25–27)

Posted July 24, 2015

*"If you ask anything in My name, I will do it."* (John 14:14)

The next four were posted in 2018:

*"Delight yourself also in the Lord, and He shall give you the desires of your heart."* (Ps. 37:4)

*"Now then, we are ambassadors for Christ, as though God were pleading through us: we implore you on Christ's behalf, be reconciled to God."* (2 Corinthians 5:20)

*"For you shall go out with joy, and be led out with peace; the mountains and the hills shall break forth into singing before you, and all the trees of the field shall break forth into singing before you, and all the trees of the field shall clap their hands."* (Isaiah 55:12)

*"Be sober, be vigilant; because your adversary the devil walks about like a roaring lion, seeking whom he may devour. 9 Resist him, steadfast in the faith, knowing that the same sufferings are experienced by your brotherhood in the world. 10 But may the God of all grace, who called us to His eternal glory by Christ Jesus, after you have suffered a while, perfect, establish, strengthen, and settle you. 11 To Him be the glory and the dominion forever and ever. Amen."* (1 Peter 5:8–11)

The next several verses were posted on different dates in 2019. I will put them in the order I received them, but without the exact date.

*"The LORD will fight for you, and you shall hold your peace."* (Exod. 14:14)

*"For if you remain silent at this time, liberation and rescue will arise for the Jews from another place, and you and your father's house will perish {since you did not help when you had the chance}. And who knows whether you have attained royalty for such a time as this {and for this very purpose}?"* (Esther 4:14, Amplified Bible - AMP)

*"So shall My word be that goes forth from My mouth; it shall not return to Me void . . ."* (Isa. 55:11)

*"Be still, and know that I am God; I will be exalted among the nations, I will be exalted in the earth!"* (Ps. 46:10)

*"All your children shall be taught by the LORD, and great shall be the peace of your children. 14 In righteousness you shall be established; you shall be far from oppression, for you shall not fear; and from terror, for it shall not come near you."* (Isa. 54:13–14)

*"I can do all things {which He has called me to do} through Him who strengthens and empowers me {to fulfill His purpose—I am self-sufficient in Christ's sufficiency; I am ready for anything*

*and equal to anything through Him who infuses me with inner strength and confident peace.}"* (Phil. 4:13, AMP)

*"Do not remember the former things, nor consider the things of old. 19 Behold, I will do a new thing, now it shall spring forth; shall you not know it? I will even make a road in the wilderness and rivers in the desert."* (Isa. 43:18–19)

*"And though the Lord gives you the bread of adversity and the water of affliction, yet your teachers will not be moved into a corner anymore, but your eyes shall see your teachers. 21 Your ears shall hear a word behind you, saying, 'This is the way, walk in it,' whenever you turn to the right hand or whenever you turn to the left."* (Isa. 30:20–21)

*"Let not your heart be troubled; you believe in God, believe also in Me."* (John 14:1)

*"Casting all your care upon Him, for He cares for you."* (1 Pet. 5:7)

*"Being confident of this very thing, that He who has begun a good work in you will complete it until the day of Jesus Christ."* (Phil. 1:6)

*"From that time Jesus began to preach and to say, 'Repent, for the kingdom of heaven is at hand.'"* (Matt. 4:17)

*"Therefore do not worry, saying, 'what shall we eat?' or 'what shall we drink?' or 'what shall we wear?' 32 For after all these things the Gentiles seek. For your heavenly Father knows that you need all these things. 33 But seek first the kingdom of God and His righteousness, and all these things shall be added to you. 34 Therefore do not worry about tomorrow, for tomorrow will worry about its own things. Sufficient for the day is its own trouble."* (Matt. 6:31–34)

*"For your obedience has become known to all. Therefore I am glad on your behalf; but I want you to be wise in what is good, and simple concerning evil. 20 And the God of peace*

*will crush Satan under your feet shortly. The grace of our Lord Jesus Christ be with you. Amen."* (Rom. 16:19–20)

*"The elders who are among you I exhort, I who am a fellow elder and a witness of the sufferings of Christ, and also a partaker of the glory that will be revealed: 2 Shepherd the flock of God which is among you, serving as overseers, not by compulsion but willingly, not for dishonest gain but eagerly, 3 nor as being lords over those entrusted to you, but being examples to the flock; 4 and when the Chief Shepherd appears, you will receive the crown of glory that does not fade away. 5 Likewise you younger people, submit yourselves to your elders. Yes, all of you be submissive to one another, and be clothed with humility, for 'God resists the proud, but gives grace to the humble.' Therefore humble yourselves under the mighty hand of God, that He may exalt you in due time, 7 casting all your care upon Him, for He cares for you."* (1 Pet. 5:1–7)

*"See that no one renders evil for evil to anyone, but always pursue what is good both for yourselves and for all. 16 Rejoice always, 17 pray without ceasing, 18 in everything give thanks; for this is the will of God in Christ Jesus for you."* (1 Thess. 5:15–18)

*"Therefore I say to you, whatever things you ask when you pray, believe that you receive them, and you will have them."* (Mark 11:24)

*"You will not need to fight in this battle. Position yourselves, stand still and see the salvation of the LORD, who is with you, O Judah and Jerusalem!' Do not fear or be dismayed; tomorrow go out against them, for the LORD is with you."* (2 Chron. 20:17)

The next verses are from this year, 2020:

*"For your obedience has become known to all. Therefore I am glad on your behalf; but I want you to be wise in what is good, and simple concerning evil. 20 And the God of peace*

*will crush Satan under your feet shortly. The grace of our Lord Jesus Christ be with you. Amen."* (Rom. 16:19–20)

*"And I will rebuke the devourer for your sakes, so that he will not destroy the fruit of your ground. Nor shall the vine fail to bear fruit for you in the field,' says the LORD of hosts."* (Mal. 3:11)

*"I beseech you therefore, brethren, by the mercies of God, that you present your bodies a living sacrifice, holy acceptable to God, which is your reasonable service. 2 And do not be conformed to this world, but be transformed by the renewing of your mind, that you may prove what is that good and acceptable will of God."* (Rom. 12:1-2)

*"I will instruct you and teach you in the way you should go; I will guide you with My eye."* (Ps 32:8)

This next verse is not actually on my bathroom wall, but I noticed it when I was looking for Malachi 3:11, which is posted on the wall. However, even though it is not posted on the wall, it has become posted in my heart/mind; it seems to come to my mind quite often so that is why I am including it with the 2020 posted Scripture listings.

*"For behold, the day is coming, burning like an oven, and all the proud, yes, all who do wickedly will be stubble. And the day which is coming shall burn them up, says the LORD of host, 'That will leave them neither root nor branch. 2 But to you who fear My name the Son of Righteousness shall arise with healing in His wings; and you shall go out and grow fat like stall-fed calves. 3 You shall trample the wicked, for they shall be ashes under the soles of your feet on the day that I do this,' says the Lord of hosts."* (Mal. 4:1–3)

Now last but not least, this Scripture from Proverbs 3:5–6 is on a plaque that is on the wall. It feeds my heart, mind, and soul every single day!

*"Trust in the LORD with all your heart, and lean not on your own understanding; 6 in all your ways acknowledge Him, and He shall direct your paths."* (Prov. 3:5–6)

That was certainly very refreshing to type and read as I was typing all of the above verses. I believe they are from the LORD to comfort me and fortify me at different times of my personal journey of life. I feel so blessed because I feel I have a clear understanding of how our Father God talks to me. I feel confident that He is with me all day long and is protecting me from the evil wiles of His adversary and His adversaries' dedicated workers. I know the LORD and my Lord and Savior are always with me and Their Holy Spirit lives in me. Therefore I am secure in my life, and I most assuredly feel "set free." And as the title of this love book says, *whom the Son sets free is free indeed!*

I pray in the name of Jesus that all my writings that you are reading will help you realize that you too are set free if you choose to believe what I have written and what is written in the Holy Bible. I pray in the name of Jesus that you have come to understand as I have. You are indeed God's beloved. Amen.

## I LEARNED HOW TO UNLOCK THE BLOCK
## & NOW I FLY FREE LIKE AN EAGLE
April 27, 2020, 9:30 a.m.

I learned key Scriptures to follow and have the block of any unbelief removed from my being. The key to living a life flying like an eagle is to believe every single Scripture that you read in the Holy Bible of God's written word of truth without fail. If you will take God totally at what His Scriptures say and not allow your mind to sway from what it says, you will receive what you have asked for in prayer; this is written in Mark 11:23–24, *"'For assuredly, I say to you, whoever says to this mountain, 'Be removed and be cast into the sea,' and does not doubt in his heart, but believes that those things he says will be done, he will have whatever he says. 24 'Therefore I say to you, whatever things you ask when you pray; believe that you receive them, and you will have them.'"* I take God at His Word and when I discover another one of His promises, I write it, post it, believe it, and therefore I do receive it! However, I do have to keep my heart and mind focused on it to keep it firm in my belief system; that is why I post it on my bathroom wall. When I see the posted pages, they immediately reinforce the Scripture upon viewing it, and sometimes even sitting and reading it again!

This is a true story that I will use as an example of innocently believing a prayer prayed over me and then receiving what the prayer person prayed for me. My eyes were -200 instead of 20/20 for years. However, when I went to a Colorado Bible conference in 2014, I sat by a young man that only came on this one particular Thursday. I had sat in the same row of seats for the first three days of the conference and usually the seat beside me was unoccupied and when I asked him why he had not been there any of the other days, he answered and said, "I am here for the Healing Thursday of this week-long conference." I said, "What do you need to be healed?" He looked perfectly healthy and fit to me. However, I hadn't taken note of the glasses he was wearing. He then explained his parents do not believe in taking the Bible literally and thought it was not logical to do so. He felt sure if his eyes could be healed to 20/20, his parents would have to believe that he had been healed because of his belief in taking all Scripture literally, especially 1 Peter 2:24, which states, *By His stripes we were healed.* The word "were" is past tense in Mark 11:23–24, which I just quoted above. I was quite intrigued, to say the least. So I thought that was interesting. I knew I was going to go up and get with a prayer partner when they called us up for healing prayer. I knew they were a team of emphatic, believing prayer-focused prayer warriors. So I said to the young man in his late twenties or early thirties, "Oh, I will do that for the healing of my eyesight as well." I had the innocence of a child as I had been wearing contacts since the seventies and did not even consider having 20/20 eyesight as normal; minus-200 had become the norm for me. So, when the end of the sermon teaching on healing was ended and all attendees had heard all the Scriptures that taught on believing and receiving what you desire to have healed, the speaker went on to explain it most assuredly would be healed if you will have faith in the powerful healing name of Jesus, our Lord and Savior who already paid the price for each believer to be healed now and forever. The conference speaker then said, "If any of you have something you want healed, come up and get with one of the many prayer warriors that will pray with you according to the Scripture written in Matthew 18:19–20, where Jesus is speaking to some of His disciples in the Bible." *"Again I say to you that if two of you agree on earth concerning anything that they ask, it will be done for them by My Father in heaven 20 For where two or three are gathered together in My name, I am there in the midst of them."* I immediately went up and had a powerful, God-fearing prayer warrior pray a prayer of healing for my -200 eye vision to become 20/20, as the eyes of Jesus are 20/20. There was more to her words, but that is pretty much the gist of it. I left believing my eyes were healed in the powerful name of Jesus. It was not too much after that conference that I found I no longer needed to put in my contacts because my eyes were—and are, still to this day—20/20. Amen! If ever my eyes do, from time to time, get tired or blurry from reading too long or with bad lighting I simply remind myself and declare out loud, "No eyes, you see perfectly well!" I then go on to something else and let my eyes rest from reading in bad lighting or for too long when I am tired anyway. I do most definitely enjoy looking across the river and seeing so many details of the opposite side of the wide river that I used to only see as blurry until I put my high-powered contact lenses on, and to that healing, I do say, "There is power in the word of God!" The key to believing the Scriptures written is to not allow doubt to come into your mind and cast it out when it does try to invade your mind or when the symptoms are not cleared up yet. As Mark 11:23–24 explains, do not allow doubt to come into your emotional heart or your mind; keep the faith, no matter what! For if you do doubt, you will do without, for it cuts the faith cord immediately!

Another quick story and Bible verse I always used at my physical education teaching/coaching job is written in Isaiah 40:31, *"But those who wait on the LORD shall renew their strength; they shall mount up with wings like eagles, they shall run and not be weary, they shall walk and not faint."* Often in my hot Florida-sun coaching job, I had to have class after class of eager-to-go elementary students, and sometimes I felt so hot and thirsty that I thought I would faint from heat exhaustion and weariness, but then power from on high would come to me when I quoted that particular Scripture in my mind and would not allow the circumstances of my weakness to take root in my heart or mind and get the best of me. I also knew to quote Isaiah 40:29, which says, *"He gives power to the weak, and to those who have no might He increases strength."* When I would say what God said through Isaiah, His prophet, I would rebound every single time. And even at sixty-four years of age, my former husband and my son's dad often says, "You need to act your age and quit jumping from the dock to the boat like that or you're going to get hurt," and many other times he tries to remind me of my age. I always ignore him and bounce around like the girl he was married to when I was in my twenties. I try to talk to him about my belief that "You are as young and spry as you are willing to set your mind on!" But he most assuredly disagrees with my spryness attitude each time it comes up. My best teaching friend at my last school also felt I had boundless energy because she did not even like to come out to the PE field to visit with me because of the hot Florida heat, especially at the back of the school, where I was always engaged in sports or exercising with my many classes of very gung-ho elementary students. Avis always made me feel loved and appreciated. I miss working with her and seeing her daily. I miss her a lot!

Dear LORD, I pray for each person reading this April 27 reading to receive healing of anything that may be ailing them, whether it be sickness, tiredness, eyesight healing, fear, worry, anxiousness, diabetes, or any other infirmity in their heart, mind, or soul. For Your Word states in Isaiah 53:4–5 that Jesus Christ, our Lord and Savior, did this for us: *"Surely He has borne our griefs and carried our sorrows; yet we esteemed Him stricken, smitten by God, and afflicted, 5 but he was wounded for our transgressions, He was bruised for our iniquities; the chastisement for our peace was upon Him, and by His stripes, we are healed."* We are healed; "are" is a present tense verb meaning this present day, if you are willing to believe, you will receive what I am asking for each of us in this love prayer. It is my heart's desire for each person reading this passage and prayer that you will, this very day, receive what our Lord and Savior so willing did almost two thousand years ago so that we all could live the life God has intended for us all along. And to this heartfelt prayer of thanks, praise, and requests I do say in Jesus' mighty powerful name. Amen!

## GRATEFUL TO BE SET FREE & BE
## A NEW CREATION IN CHRIST
April 28, 2020, 12:09 a.m.

Almost beyond words, I am grateful to be set free from my old way of thinking and living. I am thankful to be a new creation in Christ, as written about in 2 Corinthians 5:17, *"Therefore, if anyone is in Christ; he is a new creation, old things have passed away: behold all things have become new."* As the verse says, I am a brand-new creation; my old way of thinking, behaving, believing, etc. has passed away. I am now a new creation; my new way of thinking is made brand new.

I think about all things differently now. I believe in all the verses and promises written in the Holy Bible. I have most assuredly allowed this transformation to take place and the old Candy has taken on the new identity and become Candice Irene. I now associate with the ways of thinking that are in alignment with God's written word, and my old way of worldly thinking has passed away. I now have a "new normal" and I like it better than the way I used to think in my youthful years. What is considered fun to me now is studying the Word, listening to Christian television teachers/preachers, hanging out with people who strive to know who Christ is and was. I want to learn something new each day about who Christ is and what He accomplished for each and every one of us. I also want to share and continue my certified-teaching career, which is somewhat related to coaching/teaching physical education, yet different. What I mean by this is, I want to continue to teach and be a life coach on the goodness of God for as many people as I possibly can. I want to be a fisherman of people like Jesus requested of Peter and Andrew in Matthew 4:18–19 *"As Jesus, walking beside the Sea of Galilee, saw two brothers, Simon called Peter and Andrew his brother, casting a net into the sea; for they were fishermen. 19 Then He said to them, Come, follow me, and I will make you fishers of men."* I truly believe following Jesus and learning more about Him is extremely worthwhile. I want to help others learn what I have learned about the overflowing love of Jesus. I want others to know how much God loves them no matter what their past is and that He wants them to be set free from all condemnation, fear, worry, and all the other lies of Satan. I want to teach them how God and Jesus came into my life and transformed me and that the Lord so desires to do it for each one of them as well. I want to teach others how to take God at His word which is written in the Bible. I want to share all the things I am experiencing with my new lifestyle. I now have the desire to put God first in my life! I want to know and fulfill God's purpose for my life. This is what I now call fun; it is my "new normal."

The above paragraphs that are written and all the other pages of this love book written starting April 1, 2020, is how I am positive I am not the girl I used to be in my teenage years, my twenties, thirties, and forties. When I turned fifty, God started working within me and quieting my inner restless spirit enough to hear His still, small voice. I learned to pray, seek, and ask for God's help and most assuredly learned to say the quickest prayer possible, which is, "Jesus, help!" I learned when I asked for His help, I received it. This is why this days title reads as it does: Grateful to be set free and be a new creation in Christ! I am grateful indeed and do not ever long to be the way I was in my earlier years and to that change of mindset I do say amen and hallelujah! (1:11 a.m.)

## SET FREE WITH PEACE OF MIND
## BY THE GREAT I AM
April 29, 2020, 1:44 a.m.

When I woke at 1:44 a.m. this Wednesday morning, I just wanted to come to the computer keypad and thank the great I AM, which of course is God Almighty, Creator of the world. Wow, what an amazing Father God we have the pleasure to get to spend every day with, and if we choose to believe in the death, burial, and resurrection of His only begotten Son, we get to have His Holy Spirit come and dwell in us forevermore. We get to have His guidance, direction, and friendship with us every moment of the day or night. How blessed indeed are all who choose to believe!

I just want to spend the rest of my life being grateful for all that I have been blessed with in this life. Because I have come to know, believe, and honor our heavenly family, I get to live the rest of my life in peace knowing even when the world is in chaos, I get to keep my peace of mind because I know the great I AM has the whole world in the palm of His righteous right hand; as it is written in Isaiah 41:10–13, *"Fear not, for I am with you; be not dismayed, for I am your God. I will strengthen you. Yes, I will help you, I will uphold you with My righteous right hand. 11 Behold all those who were incensed against you shall be ashamed and disgraced; they shall be as nothing and those who strive with you shall perish. 12 You shall seek them and not find them—those who contend with you. Shall be as nothing, as a nonexistent thing. 13 For I, the LORD your God, will hold your right hand, saying to you, 'Fear not, I will help you.'"* Beloveds, if that does give you complete peace of mind, I will pray for you right now:

Dearest Father God, in the name of Jesus I come to You on behalf of every single person reading this and I pray for them to receive the peace of mind that you have so lovingly bestowed upon me, your daughter in Christ, Candice Irene. I also pray for the world to come to know you as I have. I did that by reading the Bible, listening to knowledgeable teachers and preachers, and writing seven life journey books. I truly want others to understand what I have received in my sixty-four years of life and have them receive it too. I want for each and every person in Your universe to come to know and trust You with every fiber of their being and every decision in life. I want them to discover if they will simply sit down, pray to You and ask for help, and ask Jesus into their life, they absolutely will receive what they have asked for. I also pray that all come to repentance, turn from their ways of solely counting on themselves, and allow You, the Great I AM, to be their everything and realize they will never be alone or on their own again. I pray for this in the name above all names, Jesus. Amen. 2:21 a.m.

# REVELATION OF WHO JESUS IS HAS SET ME FREE FOR THE REST OF MY LIFE!
Afternoon writing of April 29, 2020

My revelation knowledge of Jesus has set me free for the rest of my life! The Holy Spirit lives within me and has made me free from condemnation, fear, guilt, past mistakes, and even future ones, shame, evil influences, and all other evil manipulations. I absolutely love the Scripture that says in 1 John 4:17, *"Love has been perfected among us in this that we may have boldness in the day of judgement; because as He is, so are we in this world."* I have been set free because Jesus paid for all my sins and blotted out all my transgressions. I am grateful for His amazing act of love, grateful indeed. The Scripture from 1 John even states that *as Jesus is, so are we in the world.* When I learned that I can be as Jesus is in the world, everything changed. I pray for each of you to get this same revelation that the gospel of grace has unveiled and revealed to me. I am set free from past choices that were meant for my harm, but God turned around for my good as written in Romans 8:28–39, *"And we know that all things work together for good to those who love God, to those who are the called according to His purpose. 29 For whom He foreknew, He also predestined to be conformed to the image of His Son, that He might be the firstborn among many brethren. 30 Moreover whom He predestined, these He also called; whom He called, these He also justified; and whom He justified, these He also glorified. 31 What then shall we say to these things? If God is for us, who can be against us? 32 He who did not spare His own Son, but delivered Him up for us all, how shall He not with Him also freely give us all things?33*

*Who shall bring a charge against God's elect? It is God who justifies. 34 Who is he who condemns? It is Christ who died, and furthermore is also risen, who is even at the right hand of God, who also makes intercession for us. 35 Who shall separate us from the love of Christ? Shall tribulation, or distress, or persecution, or famine, or nakedness, or peril, or sword? 36 As it is written: 'For Your sake we are killed all day long; we are accounted as sheep for the slaughter.' 37 Yet in all these things we are more than conquerors through Him who loved us. 38 For I am persuaded that neither death nor life, nor angels nor principalities nor powers, nor things present nor things to come, 39 nor height nor depth, nor any other created things, shall be able to separate us from the love of God which is in Christ Jesus our Lord."*

The Holy Spirit of God Almighty keeps me focused on what Jesus accomplished for me, and now my veil has been removed and I am going to only live the good fruits of the Spirit for the rest of my life. I am also going to pray 2 Corinthians 3:14 happens to each of you as it has happened to me. *"But the people's minds were hardened, and to this day whenever the old covenant is being read, the same veil covers their minds so they cannot understand the truth. And this veil can be removed only by believing in Christ."* I highly suggest each of you get with a good Bible tutor, minister, start watching Christian television stations throughout the day and evening as I do so *this veil can be removed* from you as well. I pray this moment that you will have a burning desire come upon you to learn who Jesus the Christ is through reading the Bible, and this I pray in Jesus' mighty name. Amen. That's how I learned all about Jesus and how to believe in Him, and my veil is removed completely. I must say the feeling of being set free and have boldness in the day of judgment is how I enjoy living now. Family, friends, and all of the people on the planet, I want you with us and I pray you will allow our God Almighty and the truth of Christ into your hearts and minds. I do pray for this way of life and freedom from all that was written in the first paragraph from Romans 8:28–39, and this I pray in Jesus' name. Amen!

The Holy Spirit has revealed to me in 1 John 2:20 (KJV), *"But ye have an unction from the Holy One, and ye know all things."* I have an unction from the Holy One, and I know all things because the Bible tells me so, for it is written; therefore, all the wrong choices I have made and will possibly make in the future are already paid for! However, I do not feel I will make as many careless choices as I used to because I have asked the LORD, through prayer, for wisdom, knowledge, and understanding.

I have decided to receive all that has been accomplished for each of us and is clearly written in God's holy divine written Word. I am living the blessed life He, who so loved the world, provides for each of us who choose to take the Word of God's Bible literally. I do, and now the veil from my eyes has been lifted, not only physically, as my previous story explained about my eyesight being healed from -200 to 20/20, but the veil from my heart, mind, and soul. I am thankful that God's Holy Spirit woke me up to write this love book for the month of April 2020. I have been reminded of who I am in Christ Jesus. Hallelujah! And at this particular time of our global COVID-19 pandemic, I would much rather be hearing the still, small voice of God rather than the continuous news reports.

Blessed indeed are all who are willing to call out to our Father God Almighty, our Lord and Savior, and then believe what is written about God's only begotten Son so that the Holy Spirit of God Almighty can come and dwell with you, in you, and upon you. He will teach you great and mighty things and revelations that you cannot possibly fathom without Him dwelling within your heart, mind, and soul. He wants to help each one of us fulfill our life's calling. I believe the Holy Spirit of God's still small voice within our being is as important as the pump of our heart that does indeed sustain our life. Beloveds, all you have to do to pair up with God's Holy Spirit is to believe in John 3:16 (already quoted) say Romans 10:9–10 or something from your heart close to the Scripture written: *"That is you confess with your mouth the Lord Jesus and believe in your heart that God has raised Him from the dead, you will be saved. 10 For with the heart one believes unto righteousness, and with the mouth confession is made unto salvation."* I have discovered that by reading and studying the Bible, it magnifies my faith and understanding. I have faith in all the stories and examples that are written in God's holy divinely inspired book. I have enjoyed relating to each one of the Old Testament characters as well as the New Testament characters. I truly enjoy reading all the amazing stories written in the Bible from Genesis to Revelations as many times as I want to. I find the Bible fascinating and most assuredly the greatest book I have ever had the pleasure to read. I read it as if it were the greatest novel ever written. Words can hardly express how much I enjoy reading it, time after time, for it is truly the living Word of God, and each time I read it, I find something brand new that will feed my heart, mind, soul, and give me the strength to persevere in this world with love, joy, peace, excitement, and most of all anticipation of what is to come. As it says in Matthew 6:33, *"But seek first the kingdom of God and His righteousness, and all these things shall be added to you."* It certainly has proven true for me.

I plan to live Hallelujah days even in this present-day April 2020 pandemic chaos. I have received revelation knowledge of just who I am in Christ Jesus and who our Heavenly Father God

Almighty truly is. I am in a deep, loving committed relationship with Father God Almighty and our Lord and Savior Jesus. I do hope and pray you develop a loving, committed relationship with Them as well. They are amazing and so much fun to spend your life with! Amen.

# ALL IS WELL WITH MY SOUL
April 30, 2020, 9:31 a.m.

All is well with my soul and it's all because of my heart, mind, and soul committed relationship with our Father God Almighty and our Lord and Savior. Whom the Son sets free, is free indeed. I am forever set free from condemnation, worry, fear, anxiety, sickness, and all the other demonic evil influences imposed upon us. The Lord has set me free forevermore and no longer will I allow those demonic spirits to come near me or my household of beloveds. It says in James 4:7–10, *"Therefore submit to God. Resist the devil and he will flee from you. 8 Draw near to God and He will draw near to you. Cleanse your hands, you sinners; and purify your hearts, you double-minded. 9 Lament and mourn and weep! Let your laughter be turned to mourning and your joy to gloom. 10 Humble yourselves in the sight of the Lord, and He will lift you up."* I have done that and His Word has proven true. I am lifted like a balloon with helium in it all the time now. I know God as Father God and I know He is the best Father in the whole wide world. I have been reconciled to Him because of the finished work of our Lord and Savior. He did the most loving act that can be done! Jesus gave His life as a blood sacrifice substitute for our sinful life so that we could be reconciled to the Creator of the world. Blessed indeed are all who choose to believe this heroic act of love by our Lord and Savior!

If any of the creeps or co-workers of evil come near my Holy Spirit dwelling, I immediately go into prayer to my Father God and discuss the situation with Him. I will not hide any part of the problem, including something that I might have even caused because of my past sinful nature and past old heart's desire before I asked God to transform my heart, mind, and soul from the inside out. We are still working on the outside gravity pulling—I am joking, of course, to some degree. But back to the facts, God's Holy Spirit lives in me and is continuously working in me, keeping me free from fear and condemnation for they are Satan's number one ploys to keep God's beloveds in bondage of feeling guilty, remorse, sadness, etc. Worry not; God knows you better than you know yourself and once you have fully surrendered and submitted your will to be in alignment with His will, the Holy Spirit will go to work from within and redirect your old ways and old heart's desire to His heart's desire as written in Psalm 37:4, *"Delight yourself also in the LORD, and He shall give you the desires of your heart."*

God Almighty prompted me to write my heart's desires in order at 11:16 a.m. on December 24, 2013, so I did. I wrote down all of my heart's desires, and now as I looked at the list posted on the end of my hallway wall, under my son's high school graduation picture, I see there are six of them listed on that wall hanging. They have been fulfilled; and now, I know that I know, He is able to fulfill His heart's desire in my heart so I now understand that particular Psalm written years ago is a two-way Psalm. I am having fun letting God direct my paths at all times as it is written in Proverbs 3:5–6, *"Trust in the LORD with all your heart, and lean not in your own understanding; 6 in all your ways acknowledge Him, and He shall direct your paths."* That is what I have done and therefore I receive all that He puts in my path and I am willing to go in the way that He leads me through the promptings of the Holy Spirit within my being. Blessed indeed are all who are willing to ask God and Jesus into your heart for They are eagerly waiting for that simple invitation as it is written in Matthew 7:7–8, *"Ask, and it will be given to you; seek, and you will find; knock, and it will be opened to you."* *8 For everyone who asks receives, and he who seeks finds, and to him who knocks it will be opened."* I went on to read once I had the Bible opened to that passage of Scripture and read on into Matthew 7:9–12, *"Or what man is there among you who, if his son asks for bread, will give him a stone? 10 Or if he asks for a fish, will he give him a serpent? 11 If you then, being evil, know how to give good gifts to your children, how much more will your Father who is in heaven give good things to those who ask Him! 12 Therefore, whatever you want men to do to you, do also to them, for this is the Law and the Prophets."* There you have it in a nutshell: Do unto others what you would want to be done unto yourself. That also means do unto God and Jesus as you would want to be done unto yourself; just simple words of wisdom that I have learned in my sixty-four years of living and the last fourteen years have been a life spent with doing it His way and not by past-experienced ways. I now ask the LORD in intimate prayer time to direct all my paths in a way that would be most pleasing to Him. He is always a Father that leads me, His daughter Candice Irene, into paths of His goodness, mercy, and extended grace now and for eternity to come. My new life with Christ, as my example, and God as my Heavenly Father, I am experiencing a life that is, to me, the best it gets! I pray for this life of intimacy with God Almighty and Jesus Christ for all of you as well. It is in the mighty powerful name of Jesus that I pray this prayer. Amen.

# CONCLUSION
April 30, 2020, 11:15 a.m.

As I faithfully conclude this April 1 to April 30, 2020, writing, I desire to conclude with a quote from John 6:29–40, which says, "*Jesus answered and said to them, 'This is the work of God, that you believe in Him whom He sent.' 30 Therefore they said to Him, 'What sign will you perform then, that we may see it and believe You? What work will You do? 31 'Our fathers ate the manna in the desert as it is written, 'He gave them bread from heaven to eat.' 32 Then Jesus said to them, 'Most assuredly, I say to you, Moses did not give you the bread from heaven, but My Father gives you the true bread from heaven. 33 For the bread of God is He who comes down from heaven and gives life to the world.' 34 Then they said to Him, 'Lord, give us this bread always.' 35 And Jesus said to them, 'I am the bread of life. He who comes to Me shall never hunger, and he who believes in Me shall never thirst. 36 But I said to you that you have seen Me and yet do not believe. 37 All that the Father gives Me will come to Me, and the one who comes to Me I will by no means cast out. 38 For I have come down from heaven, not to do My own will, but the will of Him who sent Me. 39 This is the will of the Father who sent Me, that of all He has given Me I should lose nothing, but should raise it up at the last day. 40 And this is the will of Him who sent Me, that everyone who sees the Son and believes in Him may have everlasting life; and I will raise him up at the last day.'*"

This Scripture quote basically says to me that our only job is to have faith and believe in what is written in the Holy Bible. Allow God's Holy Spirit to guide your paths, ask for help when you feel weak or afraid. Rest in the finished work of Jesus, and the Holy Spirit will help you with every one of life's situations, circumstances, needs, etc. The Holy Spirit is in each and every believer of Jesus and will never leave you nor forsake you. You are sealed by God's Spirit forever. Trust in Him and allow Him to do the work in you that is way too difficult to do without His Holy Spirit guidance once you accept and ask Jesus to be the Lord and Savior of your life. But for sure you must desire this help and ask for it with all your heart, mind, and soul as I did. If God did it for me, He will also do it for you as well. He is love, and loves us all the same no matter what we have done. We are all His beloveds and created equal in His eyes.

I hope my little love book helps guide you on this journey that I have been led through and would not turn back if you offered me all the gold and silver in the world. I pray you teach it to your loved ones and believe in Jesus and all that is written. If you do that, you too will be "Set Free" forever. This is my heart's desire and God's heart's desire for each of my readers, my beloveds, as well as all the people of this world. For whom the only begotten Son of God sets free will be free indeed and live with Them in the Kingdom to come forevermore. I pray you get set free as I have been set free, I pray this prayer in the mighty name of our Lord and Savior, Jesus. Amen.

CPSIA information can be obtained
at www.ICGtesting.com
Printed in the USA
JSHW050542210722
28307JS00002B/160